D0384356

the BENEDICTINE RULE OF LEADERSHIP

Classic Management Secrets You Can Use Today

Craig S. Galbraith, Ph.D.
Oliver Galbraith III, Ph.D.

ADAMS MEDIA
Avon, Massachusetts

Copyright ©2004 by Craig S. Galbraith and Oliver Galbraith III.
All rights reserved. This book, or parts thereof, may not be reproduced
in any form without permission from the publisher; exceptions are made
for brief excerpts used in published reviews.

Published by
Adams Media, an F+W Publications Company
57 Littlefield Street, Avon, MA 02322. U.S.A.
www.adamsmedia.com

ISBN: 1-59337-005-9

Printed in Canada.
J I H G F E D C B A

Library of Congress Cataloging-in-Publication Data
Galbraith, Craig.
The Benedictine rule of leadership / Craig S. Galbraith, Oliver Galbraith III.
p.   cm.
ISBN 1-59337-005-9
1. Benedict, Saint, Abbot of Monte Cassino. Regula. 2.Leadership–Religious aspects–
Christianity. I. Galbraith, Oliver. II. Title.
BX3004.Z5G35 2004
255'.106–dc22

2003019612

This publication is designed to provide accurate and authoritative information with regard to
the subject matter covered. It is sold with the understanding that the publisher is not engaged
in rendering legal, accounting, or other professional advice. If legal advice or other expert
services is required, the services of a competent professional person should be sought.
—From a *Declaration of Principles* jointly adopted by a Committee
of the American Bar Association and a Committee of Publishers and Associations

Many of the designations used by manufacturers and sellers to distinguish their
products are claimed as trademarks. Where those designations appear in this book
and Adams Media was aware of a trademark claim, the designations have been
printed in initial capital letters.

Excerpts from the Rule
The selections on pages 149–175 are taken from *The Holy Rule of Benedict*, 1949 edition.
Translated by Rev. Boniface Verheyen, OSB of St. Benedict's Abbey, Atchison, Kansas.
Used with permission.

Cover photo © Archivo Iconografico, S.A. / Corbis
Interior photograph © Corel Corporation 1997

This book is available at quantity discounts for bulk purchases.
For information, call 1-800-872-5627.

Contents

Part I: The Rule of Fraternity
Lessons for designing your organization / 1

Part II: The Rule of Group Chemistry
Lessons for molding your team / 63

Part III: The Rule of Empowerment
Lessons for honing yourself / 105

acknowledgments

Writing a book is always a lengthy and time-consuming affair. At times the writing can be euphoric, coming in waves of inspired prose. At other times, it crawls, word by word, sentence by sentence. This book is a result of several years of the authors developing ideas, reading history, taking notes, and formulating strategy; then taking another large chunk of time actually writing, rewriting, editing, and then rewriting again. Throughout this process, a number of individuals have provided incredible support and inspiration. Some have helped to build the intellectual foundation while others have provided the intense personal support to push ahead and finish the job. All together they are the driving forces behind this book.

We wish to acknowledge the effort of our major professors and mentors in our academic programs: Professor Dan Schendel of Purdue University; Professor Issa Khalil of San Diego State University; and Professor Ralph Barnes of UCLA. Without the formative insight of these individuals and their willingness to mentor young scholars, the path toward authorship would never have been followed.

Special thanks are also given to our close colleagues that have provided hours of intellectual debate, sometimes lasting deep into the evening hours. In particular, Alex De Noble of San Diego State University; Gregory Merrill of the University of North Carolina; Mike Ryan of Bellarmine University; Michael Lubatkin of the University of Connecticut; Howard Toole of San Diego State University and his special wife, Leslie; and Curt Stiles of the University of North Carolina. These close colleagues and friends allowed the fine-tuning of existing philosophies and the creation of new and innovative approaches to viewing the world.

Jim Belasco and his wife, Candy, hold a special place in our hearts, both as close friends of the family and inspirations for the completion of this book. Their contribution cannot be measured in words.

The kind Benedictine monks at St. Meinrad Abbey in Indiana also deserve special recognition. Our many visits to the monastery over the last several years helped focus the direction of our ideas, and provided the first real understanding of the relevance of St. Benedict and his Rule to the modern world of leadership.

This book simply would not have been completed without the strong support and deep understanding of our beautiful family: Jacqueline, the wife of Craig who debated the ideas and proofread the words—love really does inspire; Craig's wonderful children, Devon, Scott, Stephanie, and little Oliver who just by being there always made the work a little easier; and Diane, the daughter of Oliver III, and sister of Craig who provided important words of encouragement during the inevitable down times, particularly during the unexpected turns of life.

And finally, we would like to offer our everlasting and special thanks to Nanette, Oliver III's wife of fifty-four years, and mother to Craig for not quite that long. Nanette provided the loving glue that held everything together to the very end. To her we toast the completion of this book and the closing of a chapter in our lives.

These acknowledgments are made without the important input of Oliver Galbraith III, who passed away April 14, 2002, during a preliminary revision of this book. He was strong in his love of family and friends, guided by his unfaltering faith, and pure to the principles of scholarship and ethical honor. I have tried to thank those as I believe he would want it, using his words as much as mine. No doubt I have overlooked somebody that he would like to have mentioned, and for this I apologize. Oliver had many close friends throughout the world. And while this short book will be the last entry on Oliver's professional resume, his ideas, thoughts, and memories will continue to inspire for generations to come.

—Craig Galbraith

Preface

It seems that both the best and worst of humankind emerge whenever civilization is at a crossroads. In the fifth century, Rome was at one of these great historical crossroads. Crumbling and only a shadow of its former self, the great empire was rotting from internal corruption. Barbarians from the north habitually sacked the great southern European cities. Fierce bands of thieves roamed throughout the countryside, raping and pillaging with impunity. Civilization was rapidly falling into the Dark Ages.

The memory of Rome's former greatness was still fresh in the hearts and minds of its population. Remnants of this greatness could still be seen everywhere. It was evident in the centuries-old architecture and art that adorned the ancient Roman cities. It was ingrained in the still-existing language, books, and poetry of the Greco-Roman traditions. But now the artifacts were only tangible reminders of a better time.

The world's spiritual life was also at a pivotal point. The new faith of Christianity, encouraged by the brilliant humility of its early spiritual leaders and the passionate devotion of its followers, had found its inspirational soul. Christianity was expanding its roots and capturing the heart of a small, but rapidly growing, portion of the population. The organization of Christianity, however, had not yet coalesced. The structure of the Church hierarchy, the appointment of leaders, and the nuances of dogma were still in a state of great uncertainty at the end of the fifth century.

Into this vacuum stepped a few truly remarkable men and women. One of these was a young man, Benedict of Nursia (A.D. 480–547). Born into nobility, Benedict knew and appreciated the splendors of Greco-Roman culture. But his new religion of Christianity made him reject the rotten core of what Roman civilization had become.[1] Like many of the great Christian luminaries of that age, Benedict was a man motivated by faith. Yet he also saw the necessity of establishing a practical framework for the organization and leadership of spiritual communities. After many years of leading an ever-expanding network of monastic orders, Benedict wrote his famous Rule. The Rule of Benedict was a masterpiece of leadership principles. It combined the best of Greco-Roman organizational theory with the tenets of early Christian leadership. In the Rule, Benedict crystallized practical insights from his years of personally managing an organization during one of the most difficult times in history.

The Rule deals almost exclusively with the internal workings of organizations. It focuses on proper management, motivation, and organization of daily work, and the most basic, but often forgotten, universal principles of leadership. Benedict concentrated on the true bedrock principles that motivated people of all cultures. He believed that the individual leader, under the guidance of these unbreakable basic rules of leadership, would be able to successfully adapt to the individual situation as necessary, regardless of time or place.

As a management system, the Rule has been remarkably successful and enduring. It has provided the basic leadership text for thousands of organizations for close to fifteen centuries. This fact alone speaks volumes to its longevity and modern-day relevance.

The Benedictine influence has gone much deeper than most people realize. The modern international banking system, the preservation of ancient documents, the great medieval universities that became the models for higher education in the Western world, many of our advanced farming and construction techniques, the design of modern hospitals, and the treatment of noncombatants in war are just a few of the contributions that can be directly traced to the influence of the great monastic orders such as the Benedictines.

Like the monasteries of yesterday, modern-day Benedictine communities are a unique mix of the new and the old. They live at the cutting edge of modern technology and society, but remain steeped in the deepest traditions established by Benedict and his Rule. Benedictine communities, whether for men or women, are not really part of the traditional Church hierarchy, yet they remain dedicated to its rites and celebrations. Monks are not priests or ministers, although some monks do become priests, and some priests do become monks. Rather, they are organizations of like-minded individuals.

While the majority of Benedictine communities are Roman Catholic, there are also Anglican, Eastern Orthodox, Episcopalian, and Lutheran Benedictines. There are nondenominational Benedictine orders, and there are fusion Benedictines combining Zen Buddhism with the Rule of Benedict. But no matter what century, culture, or denomination, these communities have mostly stood apart from their Church hierarchy as independently managed enterprises.

At its core, this book is not meant as a book of religion or theology. While we recognize that the Rule was written within the context of a monastic community, it is the issue of community and organization that is our interest here. We have therefore attempted to systematically distill the basic principles of leadership ingrained in Benedict's Rule, and hopefully have presented them within a context appropriate to the modern reader. In doing so we have sometimes, albeit not always, removed the specific monastic terminology and replaced it with a more generic term.

To those who wonder what can be learned from a sixth-century monk, we offer one response: It is presumptuous to act as if leadership philosophy was born in the twentieth century. Since the first tribal chieftain led a hunting expedition, men and women have been debating leadership principles. Good leadership breeds good leadership theory, and good leadership theory should result in better leadership. In the eons of recorded history, there have certainly been periods of remarkable leadership talent. Leadership theory is firmly grounded in the archives of history. As Winston Churchill once observed, "The farther backward you can look, the farther forward you are likely to see."

It is a poor general who does not study *The Art of War,* the classic writings attributed to Sun Tzu (c. 500 B.C.) or those of Prussian general and military strategist Carl von Clausewitz (1780–1831). One should question the skill of a military strategist who did not learn the lessons of Pickett's charge at Gettysburg or the Norman archers during the Battle of Hastings. In the long run, examining only recent events without understanding their historical context can only result in certain defeat.

Reading older texts can be difficult at times. Benedict wrote in the sixth century, with a sixth-century knowledge of the surrounding world. As such, the Rule sometimes references various archaic concepts, such as corporal punishment, appropriate underwear for monks, and the inadvisability of wearing a sharp knife to bed. But just as modern armies no longer throw spears and charge on horses, Benedictine communities have long ago modified these old prescriptions and tactics from ancient times.

As in the works of Sun Tzu or Clausewitz, the real resource of Benedict's Rule lies in a deeper understanding of the text, an understanding that focuses on the underlying principles and foundations of leadership. At this level, we firmly believe that the Rule of Benedict stands equal with Sun Tzu and Clausewitz in the grand body of leadership literature.

With the dawn of the twenty-first century, the management profession and the colleges of business and government that produce our future leaders must be taken to task. Surrounded by the potential wealth of stock options, preoccupied by the blinding rate of technological changes, and pressured by short-term profit announcements from Wall Street, modern leaders often choose to forget the basics. Hopefully the insights of humble Benedict of Nursia, and the inspiration of the organizations that have followed his Rule throughout the ages, will assist in rethinking the basics of leadership in some small way.

A Note on the Manuscript

There are several legends regarding the actual text of Benedict's Rule. Most suggest that after the Lombards sacked the

Abbey of Montecassino in A.D. 580 its monks scattered across Italy carrying various copies of the Rule. Tradition offers that at least one of these was autographed. Several monks, with a copy of the Rule, found their way to Rome and became associated with Gregory, later to become pope. This original, autographed copy of the Rule was destroyed in A.D. 896 during a fire at the Teano monastery.

The most authoritative known copy is Codex 914 housed in the library at St. Gall in Switzerland. Codex 914 is actually a copy of a copy of the original destroyed in the Teano fire. Charlemagne commissioned the first copy; two monks, Grimault and Totto at the monastery of Reichenau, copied Codex 914 from this. Grimault subsequently became Abbot of St. Gall in 841, and took Codex 914 with him to where it remains today. We have used three different English translations in this book. Our primary text is *The Rule of St. Benedict*, edited by Timothy Fry (New York: Vintage Books, 1981). Two other well known translations, *The Rule of St. Benedict*, translated by Anthony C. Meisel and M. L. del Mastro (New York: Image Books, 1975) and *The Rule of St. Benedict*, translated by Leonard Doyle (Collegeville, Minn.: Order of St. Benedict, Inc., 1948) are cited when a more succinct and vernacular translation was felt to be more appropriate.

You will find throughout this book references to the Rule and a number in parentheses, for example: (Rule, 25). The number indicates the chapter number in *The Rule of St. Benedict* where a particular quotation appears or from which a paraphrase is taken.

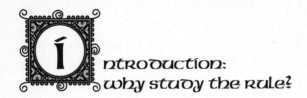

Introduction: Why Study the Rule?

Some fifteen hundred years ago, a young man from the region of Nursia in central Italy set off on an intense personal adventure, a quest that in many ways helped shape the face of the Western world for centuries to come. Not unlike the millions of similar restless men and women throughout the ages, the young Benedict probably began his quest in order to better himself, perhaps to seek his fortune, to find love, to follow more intellectual pursuits—no one really knows for certain. Regardless of his actual motivation, it was to be a personal adventure of significant and enduring magnitude.

Born to a noble family around the year A.D. 480, Benedict moved to what was believed to be the pinnacle of civilization at that time, the great cosmopolitan population center of Rome. He studied the arts and attended school. But this was the Rome of the late fifth century, the beginning of the Dark Ages, not the earlier Rome of advanced learning, political innovation, splendid architecture, and glorious conquests.

The vast Roman Empire was dying rapidly. The cities were in decay, the economy was in a shambles, and the countryside was insecure. Rome was literally crumbling around the young Benedict as invading barbarian tribes and corrupt politicians jostled with each other for power. It was here, surrounded by the decadence of the pagan world, that the young Benedict found the desire to pursue a higher mission. He renounced the material world and fled to the countryside, into the arms of a community of like-minded individuals. While there, he was responsible for the first of a string of miracles. His former nurse borrowed a sieve, which she then carelessly left on a table. It was knocked off and broke into two. Trying to comfort the distraught woman, Benedict bent down and collected the earthenware shards and prayed over them. By the time he rose to his feet, the object was whole again.

Building a Following

What little we know of Benedict's life comes from Saint Gregory, who wrote of Benedict in his *Second Book of Dialogues*. According to Gregory, Benedict soon retired to a secluded cave at Subiaco in the hopes of living out his life in quiet solitude as a Christian hermit. He would spend three years as a hermit, but even though he had little connection with the outside world, his reputation as an insightful teacher quickly spread. Soon neighboring ascetics and wandering monks were asking Benedict to be their abbot. Reluctant at first, but eventually realizing that a life of community held great promise, Benedict gave up his life as a hermit to be a spiritual leader. However, apparently he was too zealous for the group of monks, who hatched a plot to poison their leader. Benedict is said to have foiled the plan. When he blessed the goblet holding the poisoned wine, it miraculously smashed into pieces.

Benedict moved on, establishing a series of twelve small monasteries and, later, a school for children. But success bred fear. Alarmed by Benedict's growing influence, local church patriarchs and civil authorities began harassing Benedict and his new community of monks. Under increasing pressure Benedict abandoned his monasteries and moved with his followers to found what would become a great monastery upon the crest of Monte Cassino, set between Rome and Naples.

His fame continued to spread, and soon local nobles, bishops, generals, abbots, and even kings sought audiences with the humble Benedict of Nursia. No doubt they were intrigued by accounts of his many heavenly powers: He was said to be able to read minds and to make water flow from rocks. It was at the monastery at Monte Cassino, in about A.D. 530, that Benedict wrote his famous Rule, the grand document detailing the daily management and organization of the monastic community life and his principles of underlying leadership.

The Rule's Distinction

Many leaders and abbots of early monastic orders wrote rules and codes to guide their charges. Several, such as the rules of Basil the Great, Pachomius of Egypt, and Augustine of Hippo are still followed today in some communities. But it is the Rule of Benedict that has endured throughout the ages. It provided, above all other rules, the organizational guidelines and spiritual structure for the rise of medieval monasticism.

The Rule itself is relatively brief, only about fifty pages of modern text. It is divided into seventy-three short chapters, each addressing a different aspect of the daily organization and leadership requirements within a monastic community.

The Rule had two distinct but interrelated objectives. The first was to provide direction for the monk seeking greater spirituality. In this the Rule is quite detailed in its prescriptions of prayer, meditation, and daily reflection. The second objective was to guide the senior executive, or abbot, in the leadership and structure of a complex organization. With this second objective in mind, Benedict believed in brevity. The Rule, even in Benedict's own words, was meant as a guide, not to be "harsh or burdensome." He believed in the principles of behavior, that is, the basic rules of managing, working, and living within a thriving community. And he believed that principles should be short and to the point.

Thousands of Benedictine monasteries and other institutions for men and women have been established since the Rule was written, all tracing their roots to the humble Benedict and his fellow monks at Monte Cassino. Many of these communities are still in existence and flourish today, and new Benedictine orders and associations are being established throughout the world on a regular basis. The common thread that ties them together throughout the centuries is the Rule of Benedict.

Some might ask, why should the modern manager, surrounded by high-speed computers, sophisticated telecommunication devices, and highly paid accountants study such an ancient document as the Rule of Benedict? What message can it possibly provide for the modern business organization? These are, indeed, reasonable questions. We believe, and our belief forms the basis of this book, that the Rule of Benedict is an important and enduring management text that has successfully guided organizations across the vast chasm of time, from the ancient world of the sixth century to the dawn of the twenty-first. The concepts of leadership and management presented in the Rule have undergone the true test of time.

The Power of Longevity

The first reason to consider the insight of Benedict's Rule is simply the impressive longevity of the organizations it has guided. The Rule of Benedict has been the primary leadership document for a significant collection of organizations, move-ments, and communities for almost fifteen hundred years. No other document readily comes to mind that can make that claim. At various times throughout the ages, these Benedictine communities have grown and diversified, and at other times have downsized and reorganized. They have been subject to both scandal and honor, but throughout it all the Benedictine communities have always been with us since their founding in the sixth century. At one time, it was estimated that more than 40,000 organizations were guided by Benedict's Rule.

In some regions of the world, in fact, the number of men and women formally dedicating themselves to Christian monastic orders is on the rise, while in other regions, particu-larly in the industrialized West, those choosing a lifetime voca-tion confined by the monastery's walls are fewer than before.

Typical of any successful organization, however, this cycle of expansion, contraction, reorganization, and renewal is critical. This natural cleansing process has occurred many times throughout Benedictine history.

The Benedictines are remarkably adaptable and innovative. Today, many Benedictine orders of men and women are no longer cloistered and actively operate and manage a variety of enterprises, from modern universities to rural hospices. Recently, under the rapidly expanding oblate (layperson) program, tens of thousands of ordinary men and women are associating themselves with Benedictine monasteries and dedicating themselves to applying the Rule of Benedict in their daily professional and personal lives.

Why is organizational longevity important to the study of management and leadership? Because longevity is a very rare commodity in the history of organizations. Longevity is an indication of a sustainable organization or system. It is an indication of something that honestly merits intense study and deep understanding. In the literature of modern leadership theory, most of what we profess to study are really infant organizations, struggling with their first baby steps on the world stage. We generally ignore the real lessons of history.

Of greater disservice, perhaps, is that many of the corporations profiled in modern books as notable examples of superior management techniques or heroic leadership, often fall on hard times soon afterwards. Countless books, for example, were rushed to publication extolling the new generation of innovative management skills and creative leadership talent at the much-hyped dot.com firms—most of which ultimately disappeared into the e-commerce garbage bin within two years of their highly publicized public offerings. What's more, a disturbing number of the executives of these ruined and bankrupt dot.bombs are still wined and dined as invited speakers at top business schools.

Even some well-intentioned attempts to reach back into history for management insight, such as examining the leadership styles of various well-known historical figures such as Alexander the Great and Attila the Hun often miss this important point of longevity. Attila the Hun's reign, for example, lasted only a short thirty years, he was brutally murdered, and as an organization it could not be successfully passed to the next generation of leaders. Within only a few years after his death, the Huns retreated to their rural villages, never to rise again.

Benedictine communities, on the other hand, have a remarkable record of succession planning. The leadership baton has been successfully passed though countless generations of leaders, under the ever-evolving economic and political pressures of each century and the continuous march of technological innovations.

The Power of Competitive Survival

The history of Benedictine communities is not just one of longevity but of true competitive survival. At times the Benedictines had to confront hostile environments unimaginable to the modern corporation. Under historic norms, monastic communities had to be economically self-sufficient from the local Church and compete for scarce resources. In the world of enterprise they are subject to the same economic forces as any business enterprise.

Productive work is one of the basic tenets of Benedictine morality. It is an important part of daily life, and represents both a spiritual and economic obligation. Monasteries are not boarding houses, but viable and sustainable economic units. Benedictine communities produce products ranging from the famous liqueurs of France to the ceramics of St. Andrew's Abbey in the high desert of California. They plant corn, harvest apples, bake sweet breads, brew beer, design clothes, age wine, copy manuscripts, and publish books. They manage hotels and conference centers, private universities and elementary schools, hospitals and nursing homes, and libraries and museums—all subject to the complexities of the market system.

Not only do these Benedictine communities have to strategically compete within the competitive marketplace, but throughout the past fifteen centuries they have also survived a wide spectrum of overt hostile actions. Often alienated from the established church hierarchy, Benedictine orders have attracted various degrees of clerical antagonism, being humiliated at the hands of nervous medieval popes and insecure local parish priests. They have had their property and assets confiscated by cash-starved royal empires, idealistic new democracies, and Marxist revolutionaries. They have been tortured by the raiding parties of Vikings, slaughtered by the marauding armies of Islam, and brutally evicted by the SS troops of Nazi Germany.

Even the founding Abbey of Montecassino was not immune. It was sacked by the Lombards in the year A.D. 580, less than forty years after Benedict's death. The monks scattered across Italy, taking with them only Benedict's guiding spirit and copies of the Rule. Once rebuilt, Montecassino was again destroyed in A.D. 884 by the Saracens; in 1046 by the

Normans; and in 1349 by a powerful earthquake. Allied forces in World War II wreaked the final havoc on Montecassino in February 1944, by bombing the ancient landmark into nothing more than a pile of rubble. But like the enduring nature of the Rule, Montecassino was again rebuilt and dedicated in 1964.

To describe the repeated destruction and rebuilding of Montecassino, we use the analogy of a rose, which when pruned back grows new shoots. In fact, the motto of Monte-cassino is *succisa virescit,* "cut it down and it grows up stronger." The Benedictines and their influence, guided by the Rule of Benedict, always seem to survive.

The Power of the Written Text

Finally, the Rule of Benedict is a written document, essentially unchanged since the sixth century. The rule is not an oral tradition. It has not undergone any significant modification, and above all, is not subject to the whims of radical interpretation. It is a tangible document, a textual guide that can be easily passed from organization to organization and from generation to generation.

The text was written with two complementary objectives in mind. First, it is a guide to assist the monk or nun in his or her intimate spiritual quest for holiness. The Rule is filled with detailed prescriptions for formal prayer and song. It outlines the proper monastic behavior of celibacy and poverty. And it defines the daily cycles of meals and labor and the annual cycles of fasting and celebration. It is in this area, the passionate pursuit of monastic holiness, that the Rule of Benedict may seem alien and harsh to the casual modern reader. To those following the monastic vocation, however, the rule probably makes perfect sense. It provides strict order and direction in the personal quest for spiritual happiness that only those pursuing a lifetime monastic vocation could understand.

The second objective of the Rule of Benedict, and the one that concerns us in this book, is to guide the management of the organization. It is a time-tested collection of essential leadership principles designed to keep an organization on track through both the best and harshest of situations. The rule addresses leadership qualities, promotion strategies, and job rotation. It examines employee discipline, organizational integrity, and sources of innovation. It discusses retirement planning and leadership succession. Here, as a management text, the advice of Benedict seems as fresh and relevant today as it was when penned at Montecassino in the year A.D. 530.

Benedict did not write his rule in a vacuum. Like any good leader, he most certainly collected, studied, and compiled concepts and ideas about leadership and organization in circulation at the time. But it was Benedict's special genius that framed this particular document into one of the world's most enduring and useful texts. It combined the best of a thousand years of Greco-Roman practice of leadership with the basic principles of human behavior of the new faith of Christianity.

In fact, the rule has not only guided the Benedictine communities through the centuries, but it also became the underlying model for the rules of many other organizations that followed. From the chivalrous military organizations of the Knights Templar who played such a prominent role in Mediterranean politics to the great medieval colleges that provided the foundation for many of the modern European universities, the Rule of Benedict has provided the roadmap for successful leadership.

Benedictines take leadership seriously. They have to; the community is their life and soul. It is our belief that the following chapters summarize the essence of the Benedictine model of leadership. It is a system of leadership that has truly outlasted all others.

The Rule As Tool

To the modern reader, the word "rule" almost seems too burdensome, conjuring up visions of unbending authority and mean-spirited punishment. But the actual Latin word used by Benedict is *regula*—*Regula Sancti Benedicti. Regula*, as understood even in ancient Rome, is a somewhat softer concept. It actually means "straight" like a tool or pattern, a way of effectively shaping behavior or making sense out of confusion. And it is in this spirit that the Rule of Benedict was certainly composed.

These higher virtues can provide the common structure for brilliant managerial improvisation. Management technique is, by definition, almost completely situational. Technique becomes the newest planning tool, the latest financing instrument, and the most recent employee interviewing system. It is the language, buzzwords, and fad of modern business and governance. We teach technique in business school lecture halls and in MBA textbooks. We teach technique in executive development seminars and in motivational speeches. We offer professional certifications and continuing education credits in technique. But technique continuously evolves, from generation to generation and from culture to culture.

Technique in conflict with proper structure is universally discordant. Without proper structure, the application of leadership technique, no matter how modern or fashionable, will only produce the sound of organizational failure. But similar to musical improvisation, managerial technique applied with superior skill and the keen understanding of the basic structure of Benedictine leadership virtues can only result in timeless success.

To Benedict, this is the secret to sustainable leadership and organizational longevity. Do not change the core melody, but rather improvise around the edges with technique appropriate to the age and situation.

I

the rule of fraternity

lessons for designing your organization

The ʀᴜʟᴇ of Common Interest:
An Organizational Mind Meld

Listen carefully, my son, to the Master's instructions, and attend to them with the ear of your heart. This is advice from a father who loves you; welcome it, and faithfully put it into practice.

—The Rule of St. Benedict (Rule, prologue)

Benedictine organizations are elite fraternities. Most dictionaries would define a fraternity as a group of men linked by a common purpose, a basic feature one would expect to see in a successful religious order or enduring organization. But Benedict offered a shrewd twist to the concept; he believed that a well-run organization should be perceived as something special, an institution that not everyone could join. These dual concepts of "eliteness" and "fraternity" have been important keys to the Benedictines' staying power and continuing success over the centuries.

To modern ears, the terms elite and fraternity connote negative images of snobbery and exclusivity, but they also contain very positive and powerful organizational lessons. In fact, countless successful and historically famous organizations have been organized in the spirit of elite fraternities, regardless of their particular area of expertise. Examples include the Roman legions of the ancient world, the orders of chivalry and knighthood during medieval times, the powerful Medici merchants of thirteenth century Florence, and the great European universities of the Renaissance. As long as these organizations were able to maintain their common interest and exclusivity, they remained successful. Once these virtues were lost, however, the organizations rapidly corrupted and slid from fortune and, in many cases, disappeared from existence.

Clearly the term "fraternity" used in the world of business and commerce is much more holistic and generic to include all the major internal organizational stakeholders—employees, managers, advisors, board of directors—both male and female. But the essence of fraternity is still the same. It is the clearly understood and shared common interest, and the voluntary melding of the individual interest with a common interest, that constitutes the notion of fraternity. This is the key organizational virtue inherent in true fraternity.

The concept of eliteness serves to intensify fraternal ties. Elite fraternities, from the Benedictine orders to the U. S. Navy SEALS, share three common organizational principles:

1. A well-articulated and common interest understood and shared by all involved
2. Clear and distinct barriers to entry into the organization
3. A strong sense of cohesiveness within the organization

Each of these three principles are embedded in Benedict's concept of organization.

The Rule of Common Interest

When studying the Rule, one finds recurring references to the idea that members, or stakeholders, are bound together by the high purpose of sharing an important interest or mission. The starting point is a clear understanding by all involved of the primary organizational and individual objectives, which is the common interest. In the case of Benedictine communities, the individual's and the organization's focus are clearly one and the same—spirituality. In other organizations, it is quite different.

For this to happen, the common interest must be carefully articulated, perceived by all members as being important, and something worth bonding together for. And it must be clearly and thoroughly understood by all organizational members, from top to bottom. For example, Benedict insisted that for individuals wanting to join the monastic order there be absolutely no confusion about the objectives and shared convictions. Benedict stated, "Let this rule be read straight through to him. . . . After six months have passed, the rule is to be read again to him, so that he may know what he is entering. . . . Let four months go by, and then read the rule to him again." (Rule, 58)

A clear understanding by all members was so important to Benedict that he insisted that each new member personally write a short document stating his promise to follow the Rule. The novice then not only again recited the promise in front of the whole community, but the whole community "repeats the [promise] three times" themselves. (Rule, 58)

This brief ritual had two purposes. First, it firmly cemented the common organizational purpose and the commitment to it in the mind of the new member. Second, it served as a continual reminder of the organization's purpose for the older members of the community.

The Rule of Assistants

There appears to be a natural human inclination to centralize control, institutionalize triviality, and formalize unnecessary structure. These sorts of bureaucratic moves, according to Benedictine tradition, are the death of organizational flexibility and longevity.

Even the Benedictines themselves do not always listen to their own voice; the pull of centralized power is sometimes too great even for them. Every couple of hundred years or so, someone has attempted to consolidate the order into a centralized and bureaucratic governmental structure, only for it to ultimately fail before retreating to its more lean and flexible roots.

In spite of Benedict's aversion to hierarchy, he does recognize the need for staff and assistants. But the Rule lays out strict conditions:

First, assistants and staff should never add to the bureaucracy. Assistants are there only to assist, not to insert another level of hierarchy or to become pseudo managers.

Second, assistants are added only as a last resort, at just that point when the manager or staff officer cannot perform his or her job. Where is this point? In the language of the Rule, it is at the point of making unintentional "mistakes" or when "worry," "sorrow," or "legitimate grumbling" take over the office. It is never, however, to consolidate power, prompt laziness, or hedge against future budget cuts.

Mission Statements Are Statements of Common Purpose

Bearing this in mind, then, the mission statement—that misunderstood document that gathers dust in most organizations—plays an important, and very specific role. The primary purpose of a formal mission statement is one of stating the framework for fraternity and cohesiveness within a business or organization. The mission statement establishes, summarizes, and solidifies the common interests of its members. As such, mission statements should not be trivialized. Mission statements are not simply institutional propaganda but a strategic tool to build organizational morale and efficiency. They need to be focused, explicit, and correct. Mission statements also need to reflect the common interest of all members or stakeholders. Above all, these statements must represent a true promise of organizational behavior for new and old members alike.

The following chapters discuss the other two principles of elite fraternities: clear and distinct barriers to entry into the organization, and a strong sense of cohesiveness once within the organization.

Leadership the Benedictine Way

- Superior organizations are always formed in the spirit of elite fraternities.
- The common interest must always be made explicit, with no ambiguity or confusion.
- Mission statements are declarations of common interest, and must be absolutely correct.
- Mission statements must always be a promise of organizational behavior.
- Mission statements should carry no hint of institutional propaganda.

2

The ᏒᏌᏝᎬ of Selection and Formation:
Only the Best Need Apply

If someone comes and keeps knocking at the door, and if at the end of four or five days he has shown himself patient in bearing his harsh treatment and difficulty of entry . . . then he should be allowed to enter.

—The Rule of St. Benedict (Rule, 58)

People are the starting point of a sustainable organization. At its most basic level, Benedict believed, organizations are communities of people who interact with each other on a regular basis to achieve a shared objective. Spirit and mission may define the common interest, business activity may provide profit and cash flow, proper organization may provide structure, and leadership may guide, but people are the embodiment of any community.

The evolution of superior organizations starts with the careful selection and formation of individuals. In the Benedictine model of leadership, the two functions of selection and formation are made explicit.

The Principles of Selection

True esprit de corps is a rare organizational commodity, and one that starts with selection. This spirit is a hallmark of elite organizations. It is hardly surprising that such organizations always follow a carefully controlled and meticulous process of member selection, one based on both merit and desire.

Benedict knew that an organization is only as good as the individuals within it. He, therefore, had an unshakable belief in a meticulous and thoughtful selection process. By design, entry into a Benedictine community is a long and tedious process. As with any truly powerful organization only those showing a true desire, talent, and commitment ultimately pass the selection process and are granted full admission.

The Rule, for example, demands that "if someone comes and keeps knocking at the door, and if at the end of four or five days he has shown himself patient in bearing his harsh treatment and difficulty of entry, and has persisted in his request, then he should be allowed to enter and stay in the guest quarters for a few days." (Rule, 58)

In fact, this is only the beginning of the selection process. The aspirant has reached only the "guest" quarters, not full admission into the organization. The Benedictine model of selection is always multitiered and gradual. Full acceptance into the organization takes time; new members always understand that more hurdles remain before they gain full admission. But these future hurdles are carefully planned. They are not meant to be arbitrarily severe but rather a carefully designed and sometimes rigorous process of formation and acceptance.

Only the Purest Need Apply

The Rule has only five detailed managerial job descriptions: chief executive officer (the abbot), executive vice president (the prior), middle managers (the deans), the front desk administrator (the porter), and the comptroller/stores manager (the cellarer).

Of all these positions, Benedict used the position of the cellarer to illustrate managerial quality. The job is really twofold: managing the finances and other assets of the community, and physically controlling and allocating these resources as needed. Benedict obviously viewed this office as something critical to the success of the community. He recognized the conflicts of interest its power could create, not only in the potential of bias allocation and false ego, but also in the opportunity for inappropriate use and personal enrichment.

Benedict is straightforward in his recommendations on what sort of person to hire as cellarer:

- Those who have the most impeccable credentials
- Those who have a humble and nonarrogant disposition
- Those who will not play favorites or show biases
- Those who understand and follow the policies and procedures set forth by senior management
- Those who truly value and care for the corporate assets

If necessary, the office should be given to assistants so the office holder is not overworked or becomes careless, and if the office holder does not perform his or her duties properly, the penalty should be most severe. (Rule, 31 and 32)

Training for High Performance

Before a novice is fully admitted to the "fraternity," a rigorous schedule of training must be completed. The emphasis on training can be seen at any modern Benedictine community. Saint Anselm Abbey in rural New Hampshire offers a typical example. After several visits and periodic stays at the Abbey as a guest, a prospective candidate spends one month in the monastery in an "observership" program. The observer phase is followed by the "postulancy" period, during which the candidate spends several months participating in the normal work of the monastery. Surviving this, a one-year "novitiate" comes next. Here the novice receives spiritual formation from the Novice Master. Following the novitiate period is formal acceptance into the community and the beginning of a three-year "juniorate" phase, a process in which the junior member is again under the direct mentoring of a more senior member of the organization. There is no mystery about either the length or rigor of the process. The demands and expectations are stated up-front and clearly to the new applicant.

Interestingly, Benedictine communities tend to use the term "formation" rather than "training." In a subtle way, this shifts the emphasis from the mechanics of instruction to the more strategic outcome of instruction. It holds the objective of training higher than the training itself.

Training provides lessons in current techniques and skills. The Benedictine concept of corporate formation, however, is much more strategic. It's similar to what Jeanne Meister, a consultant and authority on business education, calls the "corporate university." Formation is the formal process designed to teach values and vision. It provides the metaphors, language, and skills to develop a way of thinking in line with the corporate interest. It creates a sense of employee self-development. It gives employees practice in the "core workplace competencies." And, unlike training, formation is education as to the "why" things happen rather than just the "how."

Selection and Formation Must Work Together

As humans, we each bring a unique set of skills, hopes, attitudes, and values to an organization. Under the Benedictine model, selection and formation do not stand alone. Instead they are explicitly related and formally intertwined as synergistic concepts. Thus, proper selection leads to more productive formation as effort is made at the very beginning to select people who have the right temperament to integrate into the community. But a well-designed formation process also becomes an integral part of selection as new members are continually evaluated, counseled, and examined. This intimate interplay between selection and formation can be seen in all Benedictine organizations.

A few modern organizations have learned this as well. During the 1980s, Chief Executive Officer Roger Johnson grew the Western Digital Corporation from a $20 million small enterprise to a *Fortune* 500 firm. At one point hundreds of new employees were being hired monthly. Johnson was concerned about how to integrate all of these people into the firm. In response, he implemented a hugely successful executive education program in which all new managers and engineers were required to study the mission, strategy, and technology of the company within days after joining the firm. Particular attention was given to the history of the company; Johnson hired a corporate historian who spent a full day teaching the Western Digital history. This training program served two purposes. It trained new employees in the culture and technology of the company, and also allowed these employees to see if they would comfortably fit within the Western Digital system.

To Benedict, few things were as important as selection and formation. As a result, the process of selection and formation were never watered down or diluted. Regardless of economic conditions or the whims of current management, the process of selection and formation was jealously protected and rigorously maintained. Selection standards were never relaxed. Formation classes were not subject to budget cuts. And the length of time in training was never shortened. To Benedictines, the formation process of the "corporate university" is one of the most valuable assets.

Don't Fast-Track Selection and Formation

In Benedict's Rule there is no fast track to full community acceptance. There is no allowance for affirmative action or preferential selection. From the sixth century on, each aspirant, from young to old and from former slave to royalty, has had to successfully cross the same barriers, pass the same exams, and sit for the same formation classes. The Rule demands this.

Asking an applicant to undergo the rigors and time commitment of the selection process requires the organization give something in return. Nothing is for free, not even a new applicant's unbending commitment to the organization. The superior leader always keeps this in mind.

What motivates the applicant to stick around? What inspires the novice to keep going? It is the promise of stability that was so dear to Benedict. It is also the promise of fraternity, and the applicant's intense hope that full community acceptance will be both enduring and personally profitable. The leader must make sure that these promises are always in front of the applicant, and most important, that the promise is faithfully fulfilled by the organization.

Under the Benedictine model, this process of selection and formation is specifically designed to both protect and enhance. It protects both the applicant and organization from false hopes, and it enhances the potential for melding the applicant's personal perspective with the organization's common interest. Careful selection ensures potential, while careful "formation" ensures cohesion and sustainability. The process establishes a level of personal commitment to the organization and an organizational commitment to the individual. And finally, it sets a formative pattern of progressive improvement, testing, and evaluation leading to final membership.

Leadership the Benedictine Way

- Organizations are only as good as their people.
- Superior organizations start with selection and formation.
- Superior organizations are not easy to join; true esprit de corps is a rare organizational commodity.
- No preferential treatment is allowed.
- Training is technique; formation is strategic.
- The primary motivator for superior selection and formation is the promise of fraternity and stability.

The ᚱᚢᛚᛖ of Merit and Seniority: Dual Paths of Honor

Absolutely nowhere shall age automatically determine rank.

—The Rule of St. Benedict (Rule, 63)

history is replete with individuals who displayed remarkable leadership at an early age. Alexander the Great (356–323 B.C.), one of the greatest leaders the world has ever known, was only twenty-two years old when he began the conquest of Persia. By the time Napoleon (1769–1821) was thirty he had commanded French armies, defeated the British in the Egyptian campaign, and had taken complete control of France. And at only seventeen years of age, Joan of Arc and the armies under her control captured the city of Orléans in 1429.

But older leaders also hold important places in history. The famous poet Sappho (c. 625 B.C.) was a woman of advanced years when she established her college for women on the island of Lesbos. Queen Boudicca of the Iceni was a widowed middle-aged mother of grown daughters when she led a British revolt against the Roman invaders in A.D. 61. Martin Luther King Jr. was in his forties when he organized marches in Washington, D.C. Don Benito Juarez was fifty-five when elected first president of Mexico in 1861. The brilliant General Robert E. Lee was close to sixty years old by the end of the Civil War. And the leaders of the allied powers in the second World War, Franklin Roosevelt, Charles De Gaulle, and Winston Churchill, were all in their fifties and sixties during their peak leadership years.

In spite of common opinion, hundreds of university research studies have consistently shown that age is not related to innovative capability, entrepreneurial thinking, or sophisticated decision-making skills. Talent simply does not appear to be dependent on age. Benedict knew this in the sixth century. He wrote, "Absolutely nowhere shall age automatically determine rank." (Rule, 63) To Benedict the issue of age is irrelevant. In the Rule he carefully makes the point that even the youngest, most junior member of a monastery could be elected abbot. Under the Rule, there is no such thing as age discrimination. Young, middle-aged, and old are all equal in their capacity for leadership.

How to Play the Merit Card

How is position determined then? Benedict established a two-pronged approach to rank based primarily upon merit, and secondarily on seniority. The merits and talents of the individual slated for a position have to be crystal clear to both the leader and the organization in general. Likewise, the merits and talents have to be superlative and overriding, particularly if a junior individual is to be promoted over more senior members. Anything less lends itself to charges of favoritism and nepotism.

In the monastic community, for example, the Rule states that middle managers should be appointed because they are wise and ethical, can share counsel with the senior executive, and because they have superior management skills. Other positions of authority and responsibility are to be staffed based upon merit and suitability for the job.

Benedict makes an interesting observation regarding the second in command. The Rule specifically states that all managers, including the second in command, should be appointed by the senior executive and serve at his pleasure. Evidently in some communities at the time, both the senior executive (the abbot) and the second in command (the prior) were elected or appointed by the same people. A similar analogy can be seen in many modern corporations where the board of directors appoints two or more executives, each with different responsibilities, to run the company.

To Benedict, this was a formula for disaster. He argued, "It is easy to see what an absurd arrangement this is, because from the very first moment of his appointment as [second in command] he is given grounds for pride, as these thoughts suggest to him that he is exempt from the [senior executive's] authority, 'after all, you were made second in command by the same men who made the [senior executive].'" (Rule, 65)

Benedict believed this was an open invitation to envy, quarrel, slander, and rivalry. Dual appointments create a natural desire to pursue discord. Rather, Benedict argued that all managers, from the second in command to the lowest supervisor, ultimately be appointed by the senior executive, and that all appointments of leadership be based upon merit and skill.

Where Seniority Fits In

But there is a parallel concept of rank, which is based upon the notion of seniority. Once the major positions were filled on the basis of merit, Benedict saw great value in maintaining a sense of rank by seniority in the organization. The Rule states, for example, "Someone who came to the community at the second hour of the day must recognize that he is junior to someone who came at the first hour, regardless of age or distinction." (Rule, 63) Where merit and talent are the brains of a cohesive organization, seniority is its backbone.

Institutionalizing seniority does several important things:

First, seniority encourages long-term commitment to the organization. It provides a powerful incentive, an opportunity to gain respect and status by simply making an honest commitment.

Second, seniority honors this commitment. A less senior member is continually reminded of the importance of commitment. The values of commitment, longevity, and sustainability are always in the forefront. For example, senior monks are sometimes called "fully formed," a title of respect and honor.

Third, seniority institutionalizes organizational continuity. Organizations evolve, expand, and diversify. Old members retire, and new members join. Within this ever-changing environment seniority provides an important reference point for continuity. Senior members are the tribal historians; they provide the oral traditions of successes and failures, the lessons of honor and scandal.

Fourth, seniority provides an explicit measure for experience. A smart young officer, while still skilled and trained, will always seek out the tough battle-seasoned sergeant for advice. Senior members have already traversed the organizational learning curve, and if called upon, can transfer this knowledge to newer members.

And fifth, seniority provides an established and recognized political system. To some extent, seniority can preempt destructive organizational politics. It can often save the organization from backstabbing and backroom dealing by cliques.

Balance the Power of Merit and Seniority

Benedict clearly recognized the danger of falling into a pure seniority system. Seniority without merit and talent simply becomes a stagnant union shop. Thus, every time the Rule discusses seniority, Benedict also carefully reminds the reader of the importance of merit. Merit and seniority serve dual but complementary organizational roles.

Under the Rule, talent and skill constitute the organizational intellect. Rewards based upon merit will always provide the creative and entrepreneurial power of an organization. Indeed, under the Benedictine model, clear and overriding merit alone should determine the positions of leadership, management, and responsibility. Parallel to this, however, seniority is carefully honored, respected, and leveraged. In true power organizations, senior members are never discarded or retired. By recognizing the tremendous asset of accumulated experience and organizational commitment, seniority becomes the backbone of the organization.

The Rule of Maturing Worker

Benedict saw a need several times in the Rule to address the issue of maturing workers, retirement care, and death within the community. Sustaining cohesiveness requires balancing the principles of organizational stability with the imperatives of productivity and organizational life. Obviously, in a monastic community older and feeble monks would not be cast out and expected to fend for themselves. But the issue goes well beyond this, to the heart of relating the cycle of human life to the organizations in which we work.

Superior organizations always demand superior performance from each and every individual, and the processes of careful selection, cohesive organization, and quality leadership will help realize these expectations. But people do age and slow down over time, or can fall ill or become incapacitated; ultimately people need to retire from the demands of daily work.

Benedict makes a clear statement to the leader to "make provisions for them." (Rule, 37) As people age and mature, do not expect the same level of physical productivity and instead reduce their workload and provide additional assistance if necessary. But while workload provisions are made for maturing workers, it is clear that their role, position, or status is never diminished in the eyes of the organization. Their seniority and respect always remain intact. A good leader ensures this.

The Rule also outlines the expectations for proper retirement. In essence, the community was to take care of its own. Even in the sixth century, a full pension and program of health insurance were provided. But Benedict makes a point of suggesting there is a balance for the pensioners and the sick. He writes, "They must not distress [the organization] with unreasonable demands," but in return "[The leader] must ensure that they are never neglected." (Rule, 36)

The respect given to the retired and to their memory after death, is particularly evident in Benedictine organizations. Pictures of the deceased with short biographies are posted in the monastery, and each year the biographies are read to the assembled members of the community as a tribute. Benedict saw this respect as part of the contract of stability and the relationship that ensures cohesiveness in high-performing organizations.

Leadership the Benedictine Way

- Age is not a relevant measure of talent.
- Build rewards on the dual concepts of merit and seniority.
- Merit should always determine positions of authority and command.
- Seniority should be explicitly honored because it creates continuity and a reference point for experience.

4

The RULE of Focused and Independent Ventures: Elephants Don't Dance Very Well

Let him [the abbot] always think of the account he will have to render to God for all his decisions and his deeds.

—The Rule of St. Benedict (Rule, 2)

Benedict readily accepted the tradition of venturing, the strategy of allowing teams to spin off and manage somewhat autonomous enterprises. In fact, a case could be made that Benedict invented the concept of venturing as a way of sustaining organizational growth. If the Benedictines did not invent the concept, they were the first to employ it on a large scale as part of a leadership system. From his own experience, Benedict believed that independent venturing, focused on doing a few things very well, was an important foundation for sustainable organizations.

Benedict also knew that focused and independent venturing was correct in theory as well. The early monastic tradition that individual interests be balanced against organization goals demanded a system that allowed members to pursue their entrepreneurial passions, but within a carefully understood framework.

To Benedict, venturing demanded some measure of autonomy and a sense of ownership. Although the Rule does not directly address the issue of autonomy, by Benedict's time it was firmly ingrained in the tradition of monastic culture. Hints of this independent tradition, however, are found in several passages of Benedict's Rule, as well as in other monastic writings of the era. This entrepreneurial desire for political and economic autonomy is particularly evident in how the early Benedictines actually constituted and managed their organizations.

In Benedict's time, monastic communities were highly autonomous and focused organizations. They were, after all, the evolutionary blend of two highly independent traditions: the hermit's life of the Egyptian desert, and the persecuted religious communities of the first four centuries. By tradition, these early communities of men and women were solitary. Administratively they were independent from the surrounding Church hierarchy, even though they respected the rites, prayers, and spiritual authority of the Church. Economically, they were separate and self-sustaining "profit centers," competing alone in the marketplace against other players. And politically they were independent from the local civil authorities even though they provided critical social services, such as medical care, lodging, and welfare payments, particularly in times of famine and plague.

These early, community-based monastic groups were truly the first large-scale experiments in corporate venturing and autonomous work-team management. By formal design, the Benedictine model bonded a small group of members into a highly cohesive group that attempted to obtain extreme performance by satisfying important organizational and individual needs. They were "tiger teams" in the most modern manner of thinking, lean and self-sufficient in the pursuit of a common goal.

Benedict knew that large, centralized organizations were not sustainable; in fact, by the sixth century most of the important leaders of monastic communities knew this as well. Cohesiveness required something other than size and power, something that simply could not be found in the bureaucratic world organized by hierarchy. These lessons were learned two centuries earlier by the Pachomian experiment in the Egyptian desert.

The Pachomian "Fallacy"

Pachomius was born in Egypt in A.D. 292, a time when Egypt was still gripped in the strong vise of Roman rule. While serving as a young conscript in Emperor Maximin Daia's army, he became profoundly impressed by the charity of the Christians he met. After the wars, Pachomius decided to pursue the secluded life of a Christian hermit. In A.D. 323 upon experiencing a powerful vision, he founded villages of hermits at Tabennesi and Phbew, both in the upper Nile region.

Pachomius was highly charismatic and had the dynamism to attract disciples and followers. Soon hundreds, then thousands of people flocked to him. They came from far and near, from Egypt, Palestine, and beyond. At first, Pachomuis took a hands-off approach to his growing flock, but soon beggars, charlatans, and thieves started to infiltrate the community. After these early setbacks it became obvious that a more active management system was needed. Over the next two years, Pachomius carefully molded the quickly expanding community into one of the most sophisticated economic and spiritual organizations of its time. At its peak, approximately 15,000 monks and nuns lived in the community, although one chronicler of the time, Jerome, optimistically reported some 50,000 inhabitants. Regardless of the actual numbers, it was a very large enterprise for the day, with its own laws, rules, and complex management structure.

The Pachomian village was organized into different "houses," each representing a particular profession of about forty people. There were houses of cobblers, houses of bakers, and houses of clothes makers. Each house had a superior and second in command. Four houses were then organized into a "tribe," with each tribe managed by another executive and staff personnel. Ten tribes made a monastery, which had an abbot and several junior executives. And twelve monasteries then made the "order," which was headed by Pachomius and his support staff.

By all standards it was a large and diversified conglomerate, managed by a clearly delineated hierarchy of multiple management levels. On the surface, it seemed like a magnificent beginning, a well-ordered structure that hinted of corporations of today. However, problems arose as less inspired members came into the community. Slowly cliques began to form, but under the inspired leadership of Pachomius it all hung together. Then Pachomius suddenly died in A.D. 346, at age fifty-four, a victim of the plague.

All attempts to institute a successor failed miserably. Like a hot fire in dried pine needles, the community enjoyed explosive growth at its peak, then quickly expired when the inspirational fuel provided by Pachomius was expended. After his death, opposition groups sprang up, factions fought, and by A.D. 387 the order completely disintegrated, its members scattering across the desert.

Benedict learned from Pachomius's example. While Benedict was certainly inspired by the spirituality and charisma of Pachomius,[1] he carefully avoided his organizational mistakes. The utter collapse of the Pachomian Order made a deep and lasting impression on Benedict's ideas about leadership and organization. He became determined not to make the same mistakes.

Benedict's Vision: Stay Lean and Flexible

Benedict's vision of a sustainable organization was one that was lean and self-sufficient. He saw the roots of cohesion in flexibility and decentralization. Modern large corporations have often been likened to slow, lumbering elephants. As a result, executives and consultants regularly dream up new ways of making these corporate elephants "dance." Benedict's response would be that while one can occasionally get the "elephant to dance," why start with an elephant in the first place? That was the lesson of Pachomius's failed system, what Benedict outlined in his Rule, and what has sustained Benedictine communities for fifteen centuries after Benedict's death.

Since the days of Benedict, monastic communities have fought vigorously to maintain this autonomy. At various times throughout history, they have battled the antagonism and control of the papal hierarchy, withstood the attacks of medieval Protestant reformation, and lost their land and property to unsympathetic governments. On most occasions this autonomy has worked to their advantage, but at times it has nearly led to their destruction.

Benedict, as well as many of the early thinkers of monastic traditions, knew that autonomy ultimately represented the fundamental key to their longevity. It allowed for the delicate balancing between individual needs and organizational objectives. It powered the Benedictines' remarkable adaptability to changing conditions and created the structural basis for entrepreneurial thought. And above all, it helped maintain their focus.

Benedict's writings reflect this entrepreneurial culture of corporate venturing. To him, the senior executive, or abbot, was fully responsible for his charges and the success of the community, and in a sense, should report only to God. As Benedict noted, "[The leader] must, above all, keep this rule in every particular, so that when he has ministered well he will hear from the Lord." (Rule, 64)

What is most significant is who the Rule ignores. The community's leader does not report to anyone in the Church hierarchy, neither to the local bishop or patriarch, nor to the local priest or minister. The community's leader does not even formally report to another monastery, even when that other monastery is the parent community.

The temporal chain of command essentially ends with the group's senior executive, a leader who draws his mandate to manage from the team yet still retains significant power and autonomy. While the source of power comes from the organization, the burden of leadership responsibility falls squarely upon the senior executive's shoulders. The ultimate standard of the leader's authority was contained in the precepts of the Rule, not because he or she simply received an executive appointment from a still higher executive.

Levels of Hierarchy: The Rule of Three

Benedict is wary of bloated hierarchies. The Rule recommends, at most, only three levels of administrative hierarchy: the chief executive officer (the abbot); the executive vice president or second in command (the provost); and one level of middle management (the deans). Certain staff positions are also suggested, such as the comptroller (the cellarer), the front desk administrator (the porter), and the kitchen manager. In addition, a small number of helpers and assistants are recommended, if needed.

How small or large should an organization be? The Rule doesn't say. But given only three levels of hierarchy plus a small support staff, and Benedict's insistence upon the senior executive knowing everyone in the organization, a highly efficient organization would probably comprise about 100 to 200 individuals.

Once this size limit is reached, new communities or organizations should be spun off, according to Benedict's thinking, with each new venture ranging between ten to twenty people. Following the spiritual principle of the original disciples, Benedict believed that twelve was the ideal venture team size, the starting point for a new entrepreneurial foundation. It allowed for a comfortable critical mass but substantial room for expansion. This entrepreneurial theme of small, autonomous venturing became the dominant Benedictine model throughout the centuries. It was, however, not always followed with care.

The Folly of Cluny

Throughout the ages, whenever Benedictine communities seemed to get in trouble, it can usually be traced to the "Pachomian" problem of growing too large, too fast, with too much centralization. For example, in the tenth century, the Church started consolidating its power, encouraging the centralization of all Benedictines at the French monastery of Cluny. While Cluny was Benedictine in name, it was, in fact, very un-Benedictine-like.

The idea was to set up Cluny as the great mother monastery, the managerial pinnacle of a grand Benedictine Order. Individual communities were to act as dependent subsidiaries. It was a vast feudal hierarchy, anointed and controlled by the abbot master at Cluny, with all subordinate community abbots directly appointed by the powers seated in Cluny. The individual monks would act as the foot soldiers of the new spiritual fiefdom. Cluny harked back to Pachomius's grand Egyptian experiment, exactly what Benedict had tried to avoid.

Cluny quickly developed a pomp and ceremony that rivaled the papal court in Rome. Bureaucracy became rampant, and the restrictive centralized structure soon crushed any signs of entrepreneurial initiative from the now hundreds of subordinate communities. The problem was not really with the spirituality and sanctity of Cluny; for the most part, it was quite strict and honorable. Rather the defect was with structure and leadership. It was the business model of Cluny that was terribly misguided.

Reaction against the centralized command at Cluny was swift. By the eleventh century, small groups of Benedictine reformists started splitting off, desiring to return to their earlier Benedictine roots. The resulting Camaldolese, Carthusian, Cistercian, and other reformist foundations were all established under the traditional notion that each community was a separate cohesive family, politically and economically independent from others.

Cluny soon collapsed under its own institutional weight, leaving only the reformist communities to carry on the Benedictine tradition. Cardinal Richelieu, of *Three Musketeers* fame, tried to force a similar amalgamation of French Benedictines in 1634. It also failed.

Creative Destruction

This cleansing cycle of centralization, collapse, renewal, and return to the basics has occurred several times throughout the centuries. Remarkably, in each cycle the impetus for renewal springs innovatively from within the Benedictine structure, from the inspiration of its existing members rather than from an outside source. This was how Benedict envisioned it. Organizations should be kept cohesively focused and bureaucratically lean, networked together with only loose ties. The parent community of either an internal venture or a spin-off venture should provide initial economic support and assist with the early construction. But after this, the new venture essentially should be left alone to prosper or fail.

Even today this process of new venturing continues. There is no grand "Benedictine" oversight organization that everyone reports to; there is no modern version of Cluny. Rather, the common element is simply the spirit of Benedict's Rule. And while new Benedictine communities maintain certain ties with their parent monasteries, these bonds tend to be more emotional or philosophical than political or economic.

Although Benedict believed in autonomy for his communities, he also believed in respecting the laws and hierarchy around him. Monks could not preach outside the monastery's walls without permission of the local bishop. They needed to pay their required dues and perform a social role. This was a key to the Benedictine view of corporate venturing: fiercely independent as an outward-looking community, powerfully dependent upon each other within the community.

Small and Beautiful Ventures

This idea of corporate venturing is particularly evident in the way new monastic communities are formed. From the beginning, new communities have been entrepreneurial spinoffs from another community. Historically there are three motivations for these new ventures: a) The parent monastery grows too large to be efficiently managed and there is an obvious need for greater focus; b) there is a recognized need for something new in a different location; or c) a small group of monks wants to be entrepreneurial and break away.

Benedictines nurture not only spinoff ventures, but also internal venturing. Today, most Benedictine communities have established a number of internal ventures, each the heart and soul of an inspired small group of monks. From the Internet ventures of the Monastery of Christ in the Desert at Abiquiu, New Mexico, to the Trappist casket business at the New Melleray Abbey in Iowa, monasteries have seen the value of venturing. Recently, the Our Lady of Spring Bank Cistercian Abbey in Wisconsin proposed a 400-acre golf course, hotel, and conference center.

More and more firms are catching on to this 1,500-year-old Benedictine tradition of venturing. To the Copeland Corporation, as well as many others, small has become beautiful. The Ohio-based manufacturer is a world leader in the production of compressors, condensing units, and electronics for refrigeration and air-conditioning units. Implementing the plant-within-a-plant or PWP concept, Copeland divided its larger facilities into smaller, more focused parts. Inventory investments were cut by 50 percent, customer returns dropped by 90 percent, and lead times were reduced from ten weeks to ten days.

Leadership the Benedictine Way

- Make organizations or subsidiaries lean, self-sufficient, and focused on the pursuit of a common objective.
- Wean the spinoff, subsidiary, or plant within a plant from most economic and political bonds.
- Cultivate emotional, cultural, and philosophical bonds between organizations.
- Use only three or four levels of management at most; anything more hints of bureaucracy.
- Avoid, except when absolutely necessary, hierarchy, centralization, and bureaucracy; they are nonsustainable and nonproductive functions.

The ʀᴜʟᴇ of Innovation:
Nobody Cries over a Broken Paradigm

[The visitor] may indeed, with all humility and love make some reasonable criticisms or observations, which the abbot should prudently consider; it is possible that the Lord guided him to the monastery for this very purpose.

—The Rule of St. Benedict (Rule, 61)

Philosophers of science are fond of telling the story of a drunkard who searched under a street lamp for a key he had dropped some distance away. When a curious bystander asked him why he wasn't searching for the key where he had actually dropped it, the drunkard quickly replied, "Why, the light is better here, of course!" This method might be a fool's paradise, but it is a sloppy search process at best.

Getting an organization to think innovatively can sometimes appear like a "drunkard's search"—new ideas seem to be everywhere but where they are actually sought. Oftentimes innovation seems more like a process of random blundering than rational thought. Benedict knew that innovation was actually a result of proper management and superior leadership. The Roman Empire, after all, was built on the power of innovation. At the height of its power, Rome had the best machines of war and peace, the best roads, the best aqueducts, the best buildings, and the best ships of trade. Rome crushed its competition in war, politics, and business.

Understand the Power of Paradigms

Understanding the nature of innovation starts with recognizing the fundamental nature of organizational gestalts or paradigms, and the role they play in framing the way organizations perceive new ideas. A gestalt or paradigm is basically a set of "rules" that define the boundaries for an organization's behavior. Not all rules, however, are the same. Two basic types of rules are used to establish an organizational paradigm—real rules and assumed rules. While real rules are credible and rigorous, an "assumed" rule is based purely upon perceptions. People assume things about their organization all the time.

Assumptions are created from a person's culture and training, from the organization's symbols and rituals, and from the supervisor's incentives and rewards. For example, timing production workers with a stopwatch would likely create a perception that speed is important, whether it is or not. Assumed rules generally have a greater impact on innovative behavior than real rules because they define much of a paradigm's boundaries for problem solving.

During its growth to a *Fortune* 500 company, Western Digital Corporation understood the positive power of paradigms. Rather than having their corporate walls filled with hundreds of inspirational posters and motivational proverbs, the organization's leaders picked just two or three symbols. For a full decade, its most important symbol was a funnel showing the company's various product lines pouring through a common funnel of production, finance, marketing, and engineering.

The funnel symbol was seen everywhere—on covers for annual reports, posted on factory walls, and in framed pictures in the senior executives' offices. Better than words, this simple corporate metaphor explained a lot about the importance of synergy and technology sharing, keys to the Western Digital growth strategy at that time. At all levels it helped establish a powerful culture where employees and management alike saw the value of cooperative behavior.

Benedict's Three Creative Minds

Benedict knew that his Rule established a powerful organizational paradigm. The Rule, after all, is full of guidelines. By design, much of a monk's daily life is strictly regulated. There is no doubt that the boundaries of behavior, whether real or assumed, were firmly established in his communities. But Benedict also recognized that sustainable organizations must innovate; they must adapt to changing circumstances.

Even in the sixth century, Benedict showed a remarkable understanding of the innovation process. He recognized that there are essentially three types of creative behavior: paradigm-accepting innovative behavior; paradigm-challenging innovative behavior; and paradigm-busting innovative behavior. Paradigm-accepting creative behavior refers to creative problem solving and innovation within the strict confines of the organizational paradigm established by real and assumed rules. Paradigm-challenging creative behavior refers to attempts at innovation that begin to challenge the intellectual boundaries established by the accepted paradigm. And paradigm-busting innovative behavior are those creative ideas that substantially alter the existing paradigm, thus establishing a new set of rules.

Paradigm-Accepting Innovation

Recognizing the different types of innovation, Benedict quickly acknowledged that many innovative ideas are essentially "bottom-up." These are the insights and ideas that percolate from lower levels in the organization. He writes, for example, "The reason why we have said all should be called for counsel is that the Lord often reveals what is better to the [junior]." (Rule, 3) Thus the leader seeks out the lower-level members of the community for new ideas.

These bottom-up insights are typically paradigm-accepting innovations. In essence, Benedict recommends asking advice from those individuals working on the shop floor, listening to the lower echelons, and questioning the individuals who spend their daily hours toiling away at this or that operation. They are the ones who understand the nuts and bolts of the work environment. These are the employees who are constantly thinking of improvements that will make their lives a little better.

Of course, junior members, by their very status, cannot be expected to challenge the organizational paradigm. It is understandably hard for less established employees to push the rules. Benedict knew that the source for paradigm-challenging innovation must be found elsewhere.

Paradigm-Challenging Innovation

Challenging the existing paradigm demands a degree of organizational power. Bending the rules requires a sense of security. Knowing what to reasonably and productively improve is based upon an understanding of other possible methods.

At first reading, Benedict does not appear to encourage outside contact. In fact, the Rule prescribes that "no one should presume to relate to anyone else what he saw or heard outside the monastery, because that causes the greatest harm." (Rule, 67) The Rule also states that visitors should sit only at the abbot's table, and interact only with senior members of the community. This attitude would appear to discourage the introduction of new ideas. But Benedict, more than any of his contemporaries, also encouraged the acquisition of knowledge. He valued information and understanding. For over 1,000 years, Benedictine monasteries were the libraries of the Western world.

Is Benedict sending mixed signals? Not at all. Benedict was simply trying to formalize the introduction of new ideas that could challenge the existing organizational paradigm or push the rules. Benedict was not afraid of challenges, in fact he encouraged them. All members are to be consulted when important decisions are made, and junior members are told to humbly and patiently explain to a superior when assigned a too difficult project. The Rule supports new ideas, but in the proper format and at the appropriate moment. To Benedict, senior members need to push the rules and be the source of paradigm challenges because they have a better sense of power needed to change organizational inertia.

By design, modern Benedictine communities are not cloistered. Their members regularly attend conferences and seminars. They run businesses, universities, and hospitals. They regularly interact with the public. Knowledge gathered from these experiences is inevitably brought back to the organization. But it is always the more established, "fully formed" senior members who take on this role. They are encouraged to gently push the limits, to probe and find the boundaries for innovative thinking.

Paradigm-Busting Innovation

The final type of innovative behavior, and the key to truly revolutionary and radical innovation, is busting the paradigm. Busting the paradigm occurs when the organization's leaders suddenly see that a rule they thought was a rule is not really a rule. The old paradigm crumbles and a new one is established.

Because of the power of perceived and self-imposed rules, it is hard to bust paradigms from within. Usually it takes an outside influence—a new manager, an outside consultant, or an impartial observer who is not locked into the old paradigm. Benedict recognized the paradigm-busting power of outside observation. He wisely instructed the leader to carefully listen to visitors for comments and recommendations. Use the advice of people who have seen other, perhaps better, ways of doing things, he exhorted.

With respect to visiting monks, for example, the Rule states, "He [the visitor] may indeed, with all humility and love make some reasonable criticisms or observations, which the abbot [leader] should prudently consider; it is possible that the Lord guided him to the monastery for this very purpose." (Rule, 61) This insightful visitor may "be urged to stay, so others may learn from his example." In these passages, Benedict probably had paradigm-busting innovations in mind. But he also knew how this "external consultant" needed to communicate his or her findings—with humility—because no one likes an outsider telling him or her how to do things better.

Since the Middle Ages, most Benedictine communities have institutionalized these outside reviews. Each year, senior members from other affiliated communities are invited for formal visits. They discuss the community's health with members, listen to their concerns and adulations, and examine the community's procedures and processes. Afterward, a report is made to the senior executive. Thus old paradigms are busted and new ones created with a fresh set of perceived and self-imposed rules. Creative thought and innovation can still take place, but it again shifts to the incremental, paradigm-accepting nature. When the incremental solutions are again exhausted, it is then time for more paradigm busting. This is the nature of the Benedictine model of innovation.

Work = Process + Outcome

At first reading, the Rule appears obsessively detailed about the work of the community. Monks wake in the middle of the night to pray, and assemble at specified times during the day. Discipline for tardiness is fairly severe. But a more careful reading of the Rule suggests there is a parallel flexibility in the monk's daily life, a tremendous opportunity to pursue one's own path.

In one place when discussing the order of prayer, Benedict wrote: "If this arrangement is unsatisfactory to anyone, he may do otherwise if he has thought of a better one. No matter what, all 150 psalms must be chanted during the week." (Rule, 18) He is saying make sure all the psalms are chanted, but if you don't like my suggested scheme, figure out a better way for yourself. For intellectual development, the Rule legislates certain times for reading but keeps it open as to the reading material. The Rule simply states that the material must be "a book from the library, which should be read carefully from cover to cover." (Rule, 48) Regarding manual labor, there are certain times for work, but the Rule does not specify the type or nature of work, just "what is dictated by local conditions."

Benedict suggested that all work should have an appropriate mix of process and outcome, and that a superior leader must carefully evaluate and ultimately decide on the balance of the two. Anywhere there is not a clear and definable reason for the rigidity of process, let people use their own best judgment to determine the appropriate personal path to a successful outcome—within the norms of the Rule, of course.

Leadership the Benedictine Way

- Understanding innovation means understanding the nature of rules and paradigms.
- Realize both the positive and negative sides of paradigms.
- Paradigm-accepting innovations are bottom-up creations.
- Paradigm-challenging innovations flow from senior members.
- Busting the paradigm typically requires an outside view.

6

The ᚱᚢᛚᛖ of Ethics: Organizations in Equilibrium

Keep constant guard over the actions of your life.

—The Rule of St. Benedict (Rule, 4)

W hat are business ethics? The International Business Ethics Institute (*www.business-ethics.org*) defines business ethics as "a form of applied ethics. It aims at inculcating a sense within a company's employee population of how to conduct business responsibly." The Business Ethics Center of Jerusalem (*www.besr.org*) refers to "the value structure that guides individuals in the decision-making process when they are faced with a dilemma of how to behave within their business or professional lives. Usually the impact of that decision will be felt only in their immediate, organizational environment."

It can sound rather daunting, to be sure. But, like other saints, Benedict probably did not dwell on the subtleties of complex ethical philosophy. His view of management ethics was not to preach ethical philosophy to his followers but rather to create the organizational conditions for ethical behavior to be quite natural. It is hard to argue with that view. The Benedictines, after all, have some of the longest running experience in teaching business ethics. Benedictine monasteries were among the first to offer business-ethics seminars.

This influence is the main reason why various business programs, such as the ISA (Institut Supérieur des Affaires) business program at the HEC School of Management at Jouy-en-Josas, offer business ethics courses at a Benedictine monastery, taught by monks with business credentials. The internationally renowned business-ethics seminars at the tenth-century French Benedictine monastery in Ganagolie, near Aix-en-Provence, have become so popular that reservations are needed months in advance. It appears that at least some executives enjoy sitting down with a monk to discuss ethics.

Create the Climate for Ethical Actions

To the Benedictines, business ethics is a question of equilibrium. Benedict's charge to the leader: Balance the natural desires of individuals and the imperatives of organizational action. Thus, the leader's job is to build organizational incentives, controls, discipline, promotions, and hierarchy around the four most fundamental Benedictine management concepts: stability and cohesion, obedience and humility, fundamental equality and respect, and flexibility and innovation.

Examining past and modern Benedictine organizations, whether the early monastic communities of the Middle Ages, the chivalrous knights of the feudal period, or the hospitals and schools of the modern era, some common points for encouraging ethical behavior in organizations appear. The Benedictine model for building ethical organizational behavior can be summarized in ten action points.

Ten Steps Toward an Ethics-Based Organization

First, the ethical values of the organization are always made explicit, typically within the body of mission and vision statements, as well as in all supporting documents. Consistency in all documents is key to communicating ethical values.

Second, these ethical value statements must be well thought out and limited in number. These values are not political statements but rather the true and unbending ethical standards of the organization, and a code that everyone in the organization must adhere to. Benedict believed that sustainable organizations must have sustainable basic values, ones that do not change over time. But Benedict was also a firm believer in brevity for clear communication. If an organization keeps changing its value statements, it will only confuse the organization.

Third, there needs to be a clear and easily understood explanation as to why these are ethical values for the organization. Benedictine leadership style assumes that subordinates are rational and understanding members of the organization. A subordinate's decision to follow a set of ethical ideas must be a rational choice. The job of senior management is to make these choices easy to understand.

Fourth, members in the organization, both new and tenured, from lowest subordinate to the CEO, must be regularly and formally reminded about the ethical values. They must be "in-your-face" statements.

Fifth, ethical values are an integral part of screening, hiring, and training. Employees and organizational members naturally have a variety of personal preferences and agendas, but a properly designed selection and formation process that consistently and carefully incorporates the ethical values of the organization will do much to eliminate possible future confusion.

Sixth, leaders must set the highest example of ethical

behavior. To Benedict, there are simply no exceptions from this responsibility. Moral behavior and ethical expectations are better communicated by exemplary behavior than by managerial edicts.

Seventh, there must be unwavering equality in enforcing ethical rules and moral standards. Seniority of position does not create differences in expectation or enforcement. Benedict is quite clear on this point; in fact, this sense of equality is one of the cornerstones of Benedictine longevity.

Eight, there must always be a clearly understood enforcement mechanism. Enforcement should be incremental and appropriate to the offending infraction. Severe infractions were dealt with severely; less severe violations involved less strenuous measures. However, discipline is always consistent, fair, and evenly applied. Making an example of someone is never done; it implies uneven application of punishment, rather than a corrective measure.

Ninth, the leader must design the organization so that the benefit of community membership in the organization far outweighs the cost of violating its rules. To Benedict, organizational stability, a sense of cohesion, and a well understood common objective are always more effective in encouraging ethical behavior than threats of punishment.

And tenth, while organizational forgiveness and second chances are important components of the Benedictine leadership model, ultimately the survival of the organization and good of the community must take precedence. A festering problem of growing proportions must, as Benedict's analogy so aptly describes, be surgically removed once the prescribed process of discipline has been exhausted.

Competition and Fair Play

To Benedict, there was nothing inherently evil about commercial activities or the marketplace; monasteries compete all the time in the world of products and services. The Rule, however, does carefully outline the proper ethics of competition. The ethical leader must ensure that the business practice does not involve fraud, dishonesty, or greed.

This is a particularly important concept because the Rule was written well before any strong consumer protection laws, antitrust regulations, or false advertising rules. Sixth-century markets were probably pretty tough, full of sleight-of-hand negotiations, questionable products, and unregulated promises.

To Benedict, sustainable economic units must compete under a stricter rule of ethics, not the minimum codes and laws of political legislation. Benedict employed strong language regarding the ethics of market competition, stating that ignoring these moral values results in the "death of their souls."

There is another more subtle lesson in these passages about competitive ethics and the productive "elite." Benedict was always willing to sacrifice the next day's sale for long-term sustainability. Corporate cohesion is more important than short-term profitability. Marketplace behavior must be ethical, even if it means selling at lower profit margins. This balance between short-term profiteering and long-term sustainability is echoed throughout the Rule.

Recognize the Power of "Either/Or"

Soren Kierkegaard, the great nineteenth-century Danish philosopher, was fond of using the example of "either/or" to describe the human condition. He wrote that we are, in a sense, always struggling to decide which path to follow. This constant either/or dilemma in our daily lives is what makes us human, according to Kierkegaard. It is also what must preoccupy the ethical leader.

In Benedict's mind, it is the leader's responsibility to create an ethical equilibrium within the organization, a balance that ultimately tips the powers of organizational effort and productivity toward the direction of longevity and sustainability. At various points, the Rule reminds readers that life is a series of choices. Benedict writes, "Keep constant guard over the actions of your life," and again, "Day by day remind yourself that you are going to die." (Rule, 4) It is the executive's job to create an organization where subordinates, when confronted with complicated either/or dilemmas, ultimately choose the proper path.

Leadership the Benedictine Way

- Business ethics is part of a broader management system.
- Ethics cannot be forced upon an organization.
- Realize business ethics involve either/or choices.
- The leader must create the environment where subordinates make the proper ethical choices.

7

The ᚱᚢᛚᛖ of Stability: Finding a Happy Home

When he [the new member] is to be received, he comes before the whole community . . . and promises stability.

—The Rule of St. Benedict (Rule, 58)

One of Benedict's great contributions to leadership comes from the notion of community stability, or in Latin, *stabilitas loci.* Prior to Benedict, monks, hermits, and other religious folk would wander nomadically about the countryside, joining various communities as they traveled. They would stay a week, a month, or a year, and then leave and associate themselves with another monastery as they desired. Benedict's Rule changed this, and thus altered the direction of Western monasticism.

The statement of stability was made clear to each and every new member: "If after due reflection he promises to observe everything, and obey commands given to him, let him be received into the community. But he must be aware that, as the law of the rule establishes, from this day he is no longer free to leave." (Rule, 58)

Stable organizations provide continuity—continuity in leadership succession, in organizational ideals and culture, and in job security. By asking members to take this special vow of stability, these organizations instill intense commitment in its members.

From the Family Grows Organizational Stability

The concept of stability was not new to Benedict. *Stabilitas loci* was a well established tradition of organization and leadership during the peak of Roman culture. A strong military was built upon the legionnaire's lifelong commitment to his legion, and a strong politic was built upon the senator's lifelong commitment to the Senate. Such commitment helped build the empire.

This grand tradition of organizational stability was a natural outgrowth of the time-honored Greco-Roman notion of family. The extended family provided stability, commitment, and the primary structure of organization. Parents, children, uncles, aunts, cousins, and even ex-spouses and in-laws were all formally networked together into a cohesive organization.

Each extended Roman family had a formal head, typically an older male. The family head held enormous power over almost all activities, from marriage proposals to business contracts. Commerce was built around family ties, and politics relied upon family connections. Each extended family developed its own system of customs and governance. And just as the family head could discipline an errant son, the family head could also be punished by the state for a son's crimes.

But in the declining years of the Roman Empire, extended families began to act more like petty gangs pursuing economic rewards than caring social units. By Benedict's time, the family leader had the feel of a crime boss or dictator, not a concerned and compassionate father. Institutional and political commitment no longer existed. Soldiers, legionnaires, and generals regularly changed allegiances with the shifting power struggles. Politicians were no longer committed, being bought and sold by invader after invader. To Benedict, the virtues of *stabilitas loci* seemed completely lost.

Benedict, however, still firmly believed in the organizational power of the traditional family model. To Benedict, it provided a clear and definable sense of organizational commitment within an uncertain world. His Rule reestablished stability as a pillar of organizational power. It continually reminded the reader of *stabilitas loci*: "When he [a new member] is to be received, he comes before the whole community . . . and promises stability." (Rule, 58) And, "Any clerics who wish [may] join the community . . . but only if they, too, promise to keep the rule and observe stability." (Rule, 60)

Stabilitas loci is essentially a contract. Each individual member and the organization promise certain things to each other. The member promises to work and obey. The member expresses a desire to perform to the best of his or her abilities. And, above all, the member makes a commitment to stand by the organization, in good times and bad.

But *stabilitas loci* is a two-way street. As in a cohesive family, if the leader asks for stability from his followers, he must also provide it for his supporters. The promise of *stabilitas loci* made by the organization to its members involves community, fairness, and tenure.

Three Keys to Stability— Community, Fairness, and Tenure

Under *stabilitas loci*, the organization has to be committed to the notion of community. All members, from novices to those most senior in position, are considered members of the family. As a family, there is a sense of belonging and security. People support one another in a family, even though there are different roles, responsibilities, and levels of authority.

Under *stabilitas loci*, the organization must also be committed to the notion of fairness. To Benedict, fairness implies a sense of even-handed application of discipline and rewards. In a family, there should be no favorites. Everyone is subject to the same expectations, rules, and rewards. The Benedictine model of leadership attempts to instill a sense of family into the organization.

Finally, under *stabilitas loci*, the organization must be committed to the notion of tenure. Benedict believed that cohesive families were not meant to be revolving-door communities. In order to flourish, turnover had to be held to a minimum. Members were to be nurtured and encouraged, problems addressed and worked through, jobs kept secure, and errant behaviors forgiven and hopefully modified. Only in the most extreme situations would members be "disinherited." Anything less on the part of the leader violated the most fundamental principle of the *stabilitas loci* contract.

Obviously this appeal to stability has implications for the duration of a member's life. As Benedict wrote, "He must be aware that, as the law of the rule establishes, from this day he is no longer free to leave." (Rule, 58) Thus, employment for life is not just a Japanese management concept, as many mistakenly believe. Benedict's firm belief in *stabilitas loci* placed it squarely within the best tradition of both ancient Greco-Roman leadership theory and the newly developed Benedictine model of leadership.

Stability Is Management Credo

Organizational commitment for life, while critically important to Benedict's model of leadership, was not an absolute. It represents a management philosophy. The Rule does allow for organizational transfers, but only under proper conditions and if a certain process is followed. The Rule warns, for example, "The [leader] must take care never to receive into the community another monk from another known monastery, unless the monk's abbot consents and sends a letter of recommendation." (Rule, 61)

Often, circumstances dictated that an individual leave one organization and join another. Senior members are admitted into the community, but only based on clear and distinct merit supported with letters of recommendation. If an appropriate level of seniority can be established, "the [senior executive] may set such a man in a somewhat higher place in the community, if he sees that he deserves it." (Rule, 61)

Benedict's *stabilitas loci* is meant to be an important standard of organizational commitment, not a penalty. It establishes a condition for long-term cohesion, but recognizes the need for some interorganizational transfers and employment for truly meritorious individuals.

Market forces are also powerful, and economic conditions can ebb and flow. Under certain conditions "right-sizing" may be the only choice. But, even then, *stabilitas loci* still sets a standard for continued commitment in job location assistance, intradepartmental transfers, skill retooling, and lifelong learning.

The Poetry of Work

Novelist and poet Kathleen Norris, in her book *The Cloister Walk* (New York: Riverhead Books, 1996) described the Benedictines as the most poetic of all the religious orders. She wrote that she "often sensed the rhythms of monastic life. . . . They foster a way of knowing that values image over ideas." Medieval historian Jean Leclercq noted in his *St. Benedict, Abbot of Monte Casino* (Logroño: Gobierno de la Rioja, Instituto de Estudios Riojanos, 2001) that the culture of the Benedictines is almost "more literary than speculative." To the Benedictines, the activities of work and organization must always operate in a complex, yet rhythmic harmony. Executives are the master poets with the Rule defining the metaphorical beat and organizational balance.

It is not surprising that the Benedictine motto is *ora et labora*, which means "pray and work." They go hand in hand. One of the most basic concepts of economics, developed by the fourth-century Church fathers, implemented by Benedict in the sixth century, and expanded by both medieval and modern scholars, is that life and work cannot be separated. Work, and the application of talent and skill, helps define what a person has been in the past, and will become in the future. As the vision statement of the Marmion Abbey in Illinois states, "Work flows, and is an extension of our life." The Benedictine system of leadership fully understands this relationship.

Benedict saw the real dangers of emotionally separating humankind from its work. It dehumanizes the natural order of life and crushes the human spirit. Under the Rule, a moral obligation is placed upon managers, leaders, and executives. They have the power to enhance this most basic aspect of humanity.

Leadership the ßɛɲɛ੦ıctıɲɛ Way

- Stable organizations provide continuity in leadership succession, organizational ideals and culture, and job security.

- Stability bonds the members to a particular organization.
- Stability is a real contract inherent upon the organization and each individual member promising certain things to each other.
- Stability is a standard of organizational commitment, not a penalty.
- Stability provides the foundation for the daily rhythms of work and business.

II
the rule of group chemistry

lessons for molding your team

8

The ᚱᚢᛚᛖ of Purposeful Ritual: Dance to the Corporate Music

[Ritual] should therefore be short and pure.

—The Rule of St. Benedict (Rule, 20)

military leaders have long been interested in the concept of group cohesiveness, particularly under stressful situations such as combat. Why do some units, while seemingly holding a vastly superior position, collapse and run away at the first sign of pressure, while other groups, even though they may be surrounded and outnumbered, fight bravely against all odds? Cohesiveness is an all-important bonding process. It is the positive power inherent in the notion of "elite fraternity." It creates the sense of group "togetherness."

Cohesion is not an accident of nature, nor is it simply charismatic leadership. To Benedict, cohesion comes from a management process. Benedict said that cohesiveness can be traced to three basic principles: purposeful ritual, group reliance, and mutual respect. These three processes are ingrained in the very nature of Benedictine community and any other cohesive group.

The Rule of Purposeful Ritual

All elite organizations have purposeful ritual. Every elite group from the U.S. Military Academy at West Point to the British Marines has important rites of passage. From the Vikings to the Scottish highland clans to the Indian warrior cults, ritual was used to bind members together. Ritual starts upon entry and continues through the member's life with the organization.

Rituals also provide a powerful sense of stability in a troubled world. In the Niman Kachina rituals of the Hopi, men put on costumes reflecting the likeness of the spirit-kachinas. The dance reflects the return of these spirits to their homeland to watch over the Hopi by bringing rain and good fortune. These rituals create a cycle of hope and consistency in a world of uncertain weather patterns and the ever-present potential for starvation.

On graduation day many high schools set aside an hour for seniors to sign each other's yearbook. This can be a powerful "ritual of transformation," a recognition that friends might not see each other anymore. Years later these old yearbooks, and the faded signatures, bring back an important sense of continuity as they are dusted off and shown to inquisitive children.

Benedict himself recognized clearly the importance of purposeful ritual for a sustaining and unified community. Much of the Rule articulates the ritual of organization, the way group members are to sleep, eat, and work. The Rule also carefully lays out the nature and times of different prayers, and how they change according to the seasons. It details the psalms and verses to be sung, and by whom.

To the casual observer such an emphasis on ritual may seem somewhat obsessive or restrictive but Benedict knew how to use ritual as an agent for developing cohesion in groups.

Start a "Corporate Customary"

While the Rule provides the guiding principles for Benedictines, many Benedictine communities have what is called a

"Customary." The Customary is a document that describes the special customs, celebrations, ideals, and other standards of behavior for that particular community. It puts into practical terms the separate and unique experiences of each community.

The Customary of a relatively new Benedictine community in Indiana says it well: "This Customary reflects the collective experiences and wisdom of the Companions of St. Luke— Benedictine (since) the community's existence. It is hoped that the Customary and Constitution are living and breathing documents clarifying a Benedictine experience."

By design, a Customary is a simple document, with brief prescriptions and suggestions. Many are fewer than twenty pages and all community members are expected to read and understand the document. Benedict would probably suggest a similar "corporate customary."

The "Corporate Customary" should not only describe the appropriate customs, celebrations, and rituals, but also logically tie them to the overall mission and vision of the group. As noted in one Benedictine Customary, "Customs teach us to be community members, not only in external behavior but on a deeper level, by calming, freeing, and stabilizing our responses and creating a sense of order and security." A Corporate Customary should have the same objectives.

Types of Organization Rituals

Celebrations, ceremonies, and rituals infuse a team with purpose. They creates a sense of passion and bonding and tie individuals with the shared myths and cultural history of an organization. They celebrate peoples' service to the community, and create a sense of organizational memory. After fifteen centuries of experience, the Benedictines have developed a clear sense of important organizational rites and rituals. They include:

Rituals of acceptance: ceremonies of initiation into the monastery. Designed to acknowledge the deep sense of responsibility on the part of both the novice and monastic community.

Rituals of recognition: humble ceremonies of recognition, such as travel and knowledge. In monasteries there is recognition of accomplishments, but these are usually small, humble rituals.

Rituals of education: ceremonies involving formal reading and education.

Rituals of hospitality: ceremonies involving outreach and visitors. In a monastery these are often done at meal time.

Rituals of bonding: ceremonies designed to strengthen the bond between members. They are carefully structured to connect members with a shared belief.

Rituals of values: ceremonies to encourage particular behaviors that are the community values. In Benedictine communities, these are typically rites designed to remind members of the importance of humility.

Rituals of history: ceremonies involving key elements from the long history of the monastery, designed to keep the organization in touch with its roots.

Rituals of succession and transformation: ceremonies designed to celebrate the transformation and growth of members, such as a novice becoming a full member of the community.

Rituals of spirituality and faith: ceremonies such as prayer and readings.

Rituals of death, retirement, and memory: ceremonies celebrating retirement and death. These are almost always designed to remind the current members about the value of service, and that members, even deceased, will always be considered important to the group.

Design Appropriate Rituals

Appropriate rituals require careful planning. Benedict had several useful suggestions.

Organizational rituals should always be brief and to the point. For example, regarding the rituals of faith the Rule specifies that "prayer should therefore be short and pure" and "in community, prayer should always be brief; and when the superior gives the signal, all should rise together." (Rule, 20) Brief and focused ritual brings attention to the underlying purpose of the ritual, not to the ritual itself.

Effective rituals must be purposeful. To Benedict, rituals, rites, and ceremonies must be tied clearly and unambiguously to the shared common objective of the group or the specific objective to be achieved. A San Diego biotechnology firm where one of the authors worked had a formal ceremony that was followed whenever one of the firm's scientists published an important research paper: He or she was given a bottle of Scotch as a reward. The honored scientist never took the bottle home but rather shared a toast and drink with all the other scientists in the firm. This was an effective and simple ritual of recognition combined with a ritual of shared values, in this case the importance of teamwork. Everybody understood the meaning of the ritual, and it was brief. Benedict would surely approve.

Rituals cannot be contrived or fake. Nonpurposeful ritual always risks slipping into trivial nonsense, silliness, or mean-spirited initiation. Meaningless symbolism will not survive the test of time.

Rituals must be cyclical events and consistently applied. Benedict established a cycle of rituals for his organizations. He knew that following repetitive rituals creates a sense of history and organizational timelessness. Rituals need to be natural. They are supposed to release tension, not create anxiety. They are supposed to be joyous celebrations, not confused symbolism.

Rituals must be aesthetically pleasing. To be effective, rituals must be attractive. Benedict was careful to design his ceremonies to be pleasing to the eye or sweet to the ear. Like a piece of art, attractive rituals engage people on an emotional level as well as the purposeful level.

Benedict knew that ritual, in and of itself, does not create cohesiveness. All group rituals must be blended with other elements that create cohesion. Ritual is powerful but cannot be used in isolation from the other principles of cohesion, group reliance, and mutual respect.

Design Workable Rituals

The nature and extent of ritual, rite, and formal group processes need to be consistent with both the type of organization, and the nature of the shared common interest. A cohesive family may have a daily ritual for coming together for dinner, while a cohesive high school basketball team may have a short handholding ceremony before games. Rite and ritual should always be situational.

When Wal-Mart founder Sam Walton was alive, he often led a short cheer at the beginning of Wal-Mart senior executive meetings. It worked as a ritual—why? Because in the rural southern states, people are more used to various group activities at the beginnings of meetings, such as short prayers or songs. In addition, high school cheerleading is hugely popular. Cheerleaders are often invited to civic activities, and are a source of pride for many communities. Walton's enthusiastic corporate cheerleading probably would not have worked as well in Chicago or Paris.

Benedict discovered the importance of purposeful organizational ritual while residing in the caves of Subiaco. Observing the hermits and ascetics, Benedict noted that despite their dedication they had no ritual that provided a sense of direction. As he watched from his small cave, he could see all the other hermits struggling with their faith. Everyone ate, slept, and prayed at different times and for different reasons. There was no mutual support or cooperation given or offered, and over time disagreements grew louder and more serious. In fact, this is what inspired Benedict to establish his first monastery. He wanted to provide a common framework, a structure to bring people together in a meaningful way. Benedict saw ritual with its inherent sense of repetition as the starting point for structure within an organization.

Leadership the Benedictine Way

- Cohesiveness is the glue that binds a superior organization.
- Cohesiveness should be a managerial objective.
- Well-designed purposeful rituals, rites, and ceremonies create a sense of cohesion.
- Rituals alone are not sufficient for cohesion.

9

The RULE of Group Reliance and Mutual Respect: The Glue That Binds

Brothers should serve each other.

—The Rule of St. Benedict (Rule, 35)

 75

If you were to ask Benedict how to build and nurture a cohesive working team, he would likely offer these words: mutual reliance. Simply stated, members must learn to rely on other community members. In a truly cohesive organization this reliance is deep, intimate, and multidirectional. In Benedict's rule-governed world, mutual support and reliance on community members were ingrained in daily practice.

Benedict writes that monks "on arising . . . will quietly encourage each other." (Rule, 22) With respect to kitchen work, the Rule states that "the brothers should serve each other." (Rule, 35) In the Benedictine model, people are regularly reminded of this idea of mutual support and reliance. From the daily cycles of work and prayer to caring for the old and sick, Benedict made sure that people helped each other.

The importance of community reliance is also seen in how the Rule dictates how to deal with transgressions. An offending monk is asked to eat alone and to be separated from the workaday world of the community life. The rest of the community, for an indeterminate period of time, is asked not to communicate with the offender. Though the offender is ostracized and isolated, he is still within the community. Once appropriate amends or an apology is offered, he is readily accepted again within the daily life of the community.

Breaking the harmony within a team or larger organization or pursuing personal interests to the detriment of colleagues is always a punishable act, but the objective and form of punishment is always determined to benefit the entire team or community. The military, with its natural dependence on group cohesion, understands this concept very well. The daily activities of the drill sergeant are not meant to be abusive but to teach recruits that they cannot achieve anything of worth without the help of the group. Cohesion and the welfare of the unit must come before anyone's own interest. At boot camp's conclusion, the solider will know that he or she can rely upon anybody within the platoon. Those that continue into the elite units will find that this initial lesson is relearned time and again throughout their careers.

The Rule of Mutual Respect

In a cohesive team, mutual respect goes hand in hand with mutual reliance. In successful organizations people do things together and function as a team, thus evoking a sense of community. In any community, however, there are different jobs to be done, different positions to be held, and different personalities to interact with.

Benedict understood that to maintain the all-important group cohesiveness, absolute respect must be given for any and all members of the team, regardless of social status, job title, or station in life. In the sixth-century world of slaves and nobility, his was a revolutionary approach. True organizational respect lies in the creative tension between hierarchical power and egalitarian justice. While there were clear lines of authority in monastic orders, the community accepted people from all stations in life, from artisans to farm workers, from illiterate poor to educated rich.

Benedict's Rule reminds readers that the youngest, most junior member could be made a team leader, or an illiterate ex-slave could hold a more elevated position in the organization than an educated priest from a noble background. No other institution throughout history has been as inclusive in membership as the monastic orders. As the Rule demands, "A man born free is not to be given higher rank than a slave who becomes a monk." (Rule, 2) This inclusive nature of organizational membership and promotion was truly unique in Benedict's time; and remains one of the great challenges in modern leadership.

More than any of his peers, Benedict knew that individuals feel ownership in a project only if they also feel respected. Benedict sought to maintain this mutual respect by several methods. The Rule clearly states that all members must show respect for all other members, in both title and behavior. This respect was to be applied to not only the person, but to the job each individual performed within the group. To Benedict, mutual respect within the group started with the actions of the senior executive. By his or her actions, the chief executive establishes the accepted standard of mutual respect that others follow.

Of course, the precise methods for encouraging mutual respect vary from organization to organization. In Benedictine orders, for example, members all call each other "brother," dress in the same manner, and rotate jobs of menial service, such as kitchen work and housecleaning—all part of the call to mutual respect. Benedict calls the emphasis on mutual respect between group members the "good zeal," of the community, and an entire chapter of the Rule is devoted to this concept. The Rule demands that "they should each try to be the first to show respect to the other" and that to "their fellow monks they show the pure love of brothers." (Rule, 72)

This good zeal of mutual respect is the final agent that provides the bond for group cohesiveness. How many modern organizations are filled with the "good zeal" of mutual respect?

Building an Elite Without Class Warfare

Benedict acknowledged that certain activities of design and production have a more direct link to the corporate bottom line than others. In high-technology sectors, a company's future hinges on the innovative abilities of its engineers and scientists. At universities, professors are the ones who teach, research, publish, and raise grant money. In hospitals, surgeons and physicians make the life and death decisions.

Benedict recognized this fundamental fact but also carefully warned that a cohesive organization must think and work as a unit. To Benedict, it was an issue of attitude, not role or position. As soon as one group of individuals sets itself apart, demanding a higher level of treatment, then by definition the organization has a discriminatory class system and is no longer cohesive.

Benedict did not advocate diminishing or abolishing the role of the productive "elite." But he had no time for class distinction. It is the leader's responsibility to maintain a sense of unity, Benedict said. The leader must regularly remind the productive elite in any community to refocus on the organizational target and to acknowledge they are part of an organization that strives to satisfy all individual hopes and desires, from top to bottom.

Leadership the Benedictine Way

- Cohesiveness requires group reliance and mutual respect.
- Ritual without group reliance and mutual respect is meaningless.

10

The RULE of Discipline:
Designing a Lesson Plan

[The leader] must exercise the utmost concern for the wayward member. . . . Therefore [the leader] ought to use every skill of a wise physician and send in mature and wise brothers . . . to support the wavering brother.

—The Rule of St. Benedict (Rule, 27)

*t*hree strikes and you're out. In baseball, a player has three chances for success. Unfortunately in many modern organizations, the subordinate is given far fewer opportunities. One blemish in the mind of a supervisor, one black mark in a personnel file, and a career may be irreparably damaged. Many executives brag about how ruthless they are in dealing with subordinate missteps. Some CEOs of high-profile corporations are even reputed to have fired unfortunate employees who don't happen to recognize them in an elevator or office hallway.

Benedict, however, saw mistakes as a natural process of human development and learning; forgiveness was, after all, an important Christian doctrine. But Benedict also managed a complex organization and as such had daily tasks to accomplish, overall organizational harmony to maintain, and subordinates to manage. The tension between having to discipline certain individuals and maintaining organizational stability has frustrated leaders since the dawn of organizations.

Benedict recognized that his basic leadership beliefs of group stability and cohesiveness required a serious look at subordinate discipline and punishment. Organizational stability requires a degree of tenure, not a revolving door policy. Organizational cohesion is built on mutual reliance and trust, not fear of punishment. But subordinate infractions cannot be ignored.

The question is: How do you deal with errant behavior?

Discipline has several different meanings. The Latin word used by Benedict, *disciplina,* connotes the concept of instruction, education, and training, an exercise designed to provide a lesson in proper conduct. In this context, organizational discipline is more of a leadership process, one that needs to be carefully conceived and implemented in order to have the desired results. *Disciplina* and punishment are not one and the same, although *disciplina* may involve elements of punishment when appropriate.

The Rule, recognizing the critical importance of stability and cohesion, develops a basic model of addressing subordinate infractions—the lessons of discipline. This model is based upon four components or principles: consistency in application, the rule of four strikes, sanctions by peers, and discharge.

The Rule of Consistency—Never Make an "Example"

All members of a group are subject to the same rules of discipline, regardless of position, power, or personality. Benedict did not deviate from this concept. He believed that a good leader did not play favorites, particularly when it came to sanctions. The Rule emphasizes "the [leader] should avoid all favoritism . . . and apply the same discipline to all according to their merits." (Rule, 2) From the senior executives to the lowest employee, this consistency of discipline is crucial. It is not a person's rank, position, or status that is most important to Benedict, but rather his or her acceptance and subsequent membership into the "fraternity."

Previous Roman leadership practice emphasized the ruling class and distinctions in the application of rewards and punishments. Benedict rejected this. Cohesion is a community-wide concept in the Rule; it is not based on a privileged few. Benedict, however, also understood that not everyone is management material. Some members might always hold menial positions, others may peak at middle management levels, while a select few might become senior executives with more responsibility. Acceptance of this hierarchical nature of organization, particularly by those in lower echelons, is a realization that everyone plays by the same rules.

Leaders often destroy a group's cohesiveness by the inconsistent application of discipline. But Benedict was also a realist. He knew that friendships may develop, family members might work together, and certain interpersonal dependencies may occur in organizations, thus potentially creating conflicts of interest.

To resolve those dilemmas, he laid the responsibility clearly at the feet of the senior executives. They were expected to set the standard and overcome the natural inclination to play favorites. In order to preserve group integrity, personal relationships and deference to rank and status had to be ignored in the lessons of *disciplina* and the application of sanctions.

The Rule of Four Strikes

The great tradition of *stabilitas loci*, so important to Benedict, demands a degree of tenure. It requires an implicit agreement of bonding between the group and its members. In the vernacular, this bond implies that every individual will give the group the best of his or her abilities and 110 percent effort. The individual will support the organization no matter what, but in return should expect a second chance and assistance in getting back on the right track should a mistake or an error in judgment be made. The Rule recognized this bond of trust. In fact, superior organizations today passionately encourage this relationship. The leader is asked to be unyielding in his or her expectations but forgiving in the sequence of sanctions.

The Rule consistently refers to a four-level sequence of dealing with serious infractions, a four-step lesson of *disciplina*. In referring to senior and middle management (deans and priors), the Rule states, "If so deserving of censure, he is to be reproved once, twice, and even a third time. Should he refuse to amend, he must be removed from office and replaced." (Rule, 21)

For subordinates who defy the orders of superiors, the Rule prescribes, "He should be warned twice privately by the seniors. . . . If he does not amend, he must be rebuked publicly . . . but if even then he does not reform, let him be excommunicated." (Rule, 23)

The rule of four strikes applies to almost all infractions, including actually leaving the community and then seeking reentry, "If he leaves again, or even a third time, he should be readmitted under the same conditions [loss of seniority]." (Rule, 29)

There are several subtle lessons regarding discipline contained in these short passages:

First, the rule of four is equally applied to all, from senior managers to the lowest in seniority. Second, there is an increasing severity of sanctions, with at least the first two disciplinary actions given in private—usually as warnings. Third, the sanctions or discipline such as removal from office or demotion become public or known to the rest of the group. Fourth, the final sanction is one of peer pressure, where the basic motivation for proper behavior comes from the group rather than the superior.

The Rule of Sanction by Peers

In elite fraternities or organizations, ultimately it is community cohesiveness that shapes behavior. Leaders can create the right conditions for cohesion—this is their job—but it is group cohesion that actually encourages extreme performance from its members. Peer pressure from an organization that is highly regarded by the member will always command the greatest influence.

Benedict recognized the tremendous power of cohesive groups in adjusting errant behavior. The Rule consistently maintains that the final steps of discipline involve the organization. In the case of a monastic order, this is called "excommunication," which is a form of short-term isolation. This final lesson of discipline was a last resort. It was the objective of Benedict's Rule that warnings would provide sufficient motivation for the errant member.

The Rule notes, however, that the degree of peer pressure should be proportionate. "If a brother is found guilty of less serious faults, he will not be allowed to share the common table." (Rule, 24) "A brother guilty of a serious fault is to be excluded from both the table and oratory." (Rule, 25)

But even with this final step of discipline the errant member is not completely isolated. The objective is not meant to be punishment but rather a blunt lesson. In fact, the Rule states that the errant member should be counseled: "[The leader] must exercise the utmost care and concern for the wayward member. . . . Therefore [the leader] ought to use every skill of a wise physician and send in mature and wise brothers . . . to support the wavering brother." (Rule, 27) This final disciplinary step of isolation is meant to be used only as a final wake-up call. It maintains group harmony, uses the power of peer pressure within the cohesive organization, and respects the call for *stabilitas loci*.

The Rule of Discharge

As previously noted, group stability, or *stabilitas loci*, is a relational contract. It demands a high degree of commitment on the part of the member, but an equally high degree of commitment on the part of the organization and the leader. The Rule demands that the leader make every effort to compassionately modify the errant behavior of subordinates and provide for several "second chances." Anything less on the part of the leader violates the contract.

Even the fourth strike is not final. Even after isolation or the application of cohesive peer pressure, the Rule allows for one final counseling session and one final opportunity for change. If this does not work, then there is only one remedy: discharge and separation from the group. The Rule states, "Yet if even this procedure does not heal him, then finally, the [leader] must use the knife and amputate . . . lest one diseased sheep infect the whole flock." (Rule, 28)

Benedict's medical analogy is not by accident. Separation from a superior and cohesive organization is indeed a harsh and difficult act. It is not something to be taken lightly by either the errant member or the responsible leader. The discharged member loses an important bond, something cherished. The organization may lose years of invested human and intellectual capital. Discharge is indeed harsh and a loss felt by everyone. Discharge is truly a sort of "organizational amputation." But, as Benedict noted, in a truly cohesive group, the ultimate integrity of the organization must be preserved and maintained.

Honesty Is the Only Policy

Benedict speaks here about another theme that runs through the Rule—people are human and thus make mistakes. The leader's job is to foster an organizational climate that encourages mistakes, even serious ones, to be immediately reported, without fear of repercussion (except fair restitution).

This type of openness implies a promise of stability; problems arise when subordinates are fearful of being honest. As the Rule points out: "If a [subordinate] while working does anything wrong, breaks or loses something . . . he shall go at once to the [leader] . . . and confess, offering to make satisfaction. If he does not and it later becomes known, he shall be severely punished." (Rule, 46)

Leadership the Benedictine Way

- Superior leaders see discipline as a lesson plan, not as a punishment.
- There should never be favoritism in the application of organizational discipline.
- Cohesive organizations give second chances.
- Discipline should be based on the principle of calculated peer pressure.
- Discharge is like an amputation, and must always be carefully considered.

11

The RULE of Counsel: Stop, Look, and Listen

Do everything with counsel and you will not be sorry afterward.

—The Rule of St. Benedict (Rule, 3)

Benedict envisioned built-to-last organizations as guided by a productive team-oriented process, but with important lines of authority embedded within it. Certain jobs need to get done. There is the job of spiritual work, or *opus Dei*; there is the job of economic production and product marketing; there is the job of intellectual expansion for each individual; and there is the job of physical plant maintenance.

For Benedict, efficiently accomplishing a set of complex and diverse tasks, particularly for a large monastery of several hundred, required a blend of single-leader management structure and the cohesive dynamics of modern team management. In Benedict's mind, a team effort did not mean everyone had an equal say in all management decisions. Rather, it referred to a well-defined process of leader selection, informational feedback, and organizational interaction. Enhancing the potential cohesive power of any group demanded a sense of ownership by all members, regardless of formal position.

Create a Sense of Democratic Selection

To facilitate this, the Rule outlines a strict process for selection of senior executives. It also establishes how that senior executive must subsequently interact with the group. This process was so important to Benedict that he devoted several chapters to it.

Benedict believed that the initial selection of the chief executive officer should be a largely democratic process, with "the guiding principle always being that the man placed in office be the one selected either by the whole community acting unanimously in the fear of God, or by some part of the community . . . which possesses sounder judgment." (Rule, 64)

Benedict appears to have no problem with a board of directors electing the CEO, but only on the condition of "sounder judgment." Sounder judgment thus becomes the standard in the Benedictine model. Once the legitimacy of sounder judgment is lost in the eyes of the community, then the legitimacy of executive appointment by a select few, a committee, or the board of directors, is also lost.

Unanimity, as suggested by the Rule, is another cornerstone of Benedictine governance. This, however, is clearly an ideal target, something that after discussion and debate a community hopes to achieve. In reality, it has generally been a three-to-one majority in leader elections that has been used in Benedictine communities since medieval times[1].

Benedict also makes a point of noting that a person last in community rank could be chosen as the senior executive officer. As always in the Rule, age, rank, and seniority should be irrelevant; only the best and most deserving need apply. Merit is the foremost consideration.

Regardless of the actual approach taken by a particular order, the Benedictines kept alive the concept of community involvement and participatory democracy as a standard of organizational governance in a world where such things were completely unheard of. It was not until the forceful writings of Spanish theologian Ramon Lull (1232–1316) and the authority of St. Thomas Aquinas (1225–1274) that the full organization's participation in the selection of its leaders started to gain a broader acceptance.

Create a Mechanism for Executive Impeachment

The Rule recognizes that sometimes, even with the best intentions of the community, the wrong person may be placed in charge. Unfortunately, leaders can turn out to be corrupt, evil, lazy, and incompetent. In such extreme cases, Benedict allowed a form of managerial impeachment. If the situation deteriorated beyond repair, the Rule allowed for local Christians in the surrounding community, or the abbots of other nearby monasteries, to instigate a company coup or revolt—essentially overthrowing the presiding abbot.

Within a short time, however, it became painfully obvious that the "external impeachment" model was not workable. Adjustments had to be made. There was an obvious problem in electing abbots for life since senility and other debilitating illnesses usually accompanied old age. Likewise, the present-day Peter Principle (introduced by Laurence J. Peter in a humorous book of the same title), which states that managers are promoted until they reach their level of incompetence, is universal and timeless. Poorly qualified individuals can occasionally gain substantial organizational power. Even in monasteries individuals can rise to their level of incompetence.

Rather than relying on the local population to "knock

down the monastery's doors," an internal mechanism to deal with such issues was desperately needed. Over time, Benedictine bylaws were modified. Many of the communities evolved toward a term-limit system of office in which a new abbot was elected every five years. Other Benedictine groups have moved to a community-wide periodic review of the senior executive, with the option to renew or elect a new officer.[2]

In modern Benedictine orders, the chief executive officer is democratically elected either by the community in general or by a board of directors. Once elected, however, he or she wields tremendous power over the organization. Generally this power is exercised with the utmost humility, moderation, and discretion. But as protection, there generally is a periodic process of checks and balances.

Get Counsel but Make Decisions

Perhaps of greater significance is the role of community counsel in a leader's decisions. Benedict is specific about this, and devotes a full chapter to the subject. The Rule states, "As often as anything important is to be done . . . the [leader] shall call the whole community together and himself explain what the business is; and after hearing the advice of the [subordinates], let him ponder it and follow what he judges the wiser course." (Rule, 3)

There are several critical lessons in this quote: First, the high-performing executive does not keep secrets from the organization. For important issues the entire organization is always carefully and immediately consulted. Second, the high-performing leader explains the issue, in person, to the entire group, and then listens to all advice given in return. Counsel is an intimate and personal affair, a process from which a leader cannot hide.

Third, the high-performing leader honestly considers subordinates' thoughts, ideas, and recommendations. And he or she will come to a well-reasoned decision with "foresight and fairness." (Rule, 3) Counsel, to Benedict, is a cornerstone of superior leadership. It is not an executive public relations ploy or managerial cosmetics. Instead, counsel always starts with a presumption of usefulness and a standard of honesty. And fourth, no matter what, the senior executive still has absolute decision-making responsibility. Although counsel is regularly sought and carefully considered, decision making under the Benedictine model of leadership is not a direct democracy.

To Benedict, leaders make decisions. Thus, while the selection of the senior executive is somewhat democratic, executive-level decision making is not. The burden of the decision, and its ultimate success or failure, always lies squarely upon the shoulders of the senior executive and nobody else. Benedict is clear. As the Rule aptly notes, "The decision is the [leader's] to make, so that when he has determined what is more prudent, all may obey." (Rule, 3)

It is interesting to note that the Rule also prescribes that, "if less important business of the (organization) is to be transacted, (the leader) shall take counsel with the seniors only." (Rule, 3) This is Benedict's rule of counsel: If the matter is important, then it warrants discussion with the entire organization; if the matter is of minor importance, then form a subcommittee. No matter what, however, always seek advice. As the Rule notes, "Do everything with counsel and you will not be sorry afterward." (Rule, 3)

Do a Corporate "Walkabout"

Maintaining balance between the organization and the individuals within it is an overarching concern for a leader. Not only did Benedict require a leader to keep balance or harmony between the organization and its members, the Rule also insisted that the leader understand, at some basic level, the individual needs of each and every person within the organization. This meant that the leader had to circulate and know his or her organization. Get out of the office, Benedict advised. In today's world, this is sometimes referred to as "management by walking around and listening," where a manager or supervisor visibly and proactively interacts with staff.

A corporate "walkabout" gives subordinates direct access to the boss. People can rapidly exchange ideas and generate a high level of spontaneous, creative energy. It provides the two-way "rich, real-time information" that management thinker Henry Mintzberg says is necessary for the modern manager. In the language of the Rule, this means "[the leader] must so accommodate and adapt himself to each one's character and intelligence." (Rule, 2) Harvard Business School Professor Wickham Skinner called this unique ability to adjust to the personalities of subordinates while maintaining certain core values, the key qualities of "managers with impact."

Leadership the ᏰᎬᏁᎬᎠᎥᏟᎿᎥᏁᎬ Way

- Executive appointments should be viewed within the context of organizational democracy.

- Sounder judgment is the standard of legitimacy for committee or board appointment of a senior executive.
- Leadership is up-front, personal, and two-way; superior leaders do not hide.
- Executive decisions are always based on counsel.
- Important decisions require counsel of all; minor decisions require counsel of few.
- Final and ultimate responsibility for all decisions falls on the shoulders of the senior executive.

12

The RULE of Grumbling:
Measuring the Pulse of Community Health

The abbot should so regulate and arrange all matters [so that] the brothers may go about their activities without justifiable grumbling.

—The Rule of St. Benedict (Rule, 41)

If there were water coolers in the ancient monasteries, that's probably where you would have found Benedict. He had a keen ear for the barbs of discontent and sounds of exasperation, the sorts of grumbling that are early warning indicators that something is not quite right.

The buzz you hear within a group is a vital sign of whether or not the system is working properly. Vital signs are critical to understanding and monitoring the health of any complex system. They are the shortcuts that avoid a full and expensive analysis. Vital signs within normal parameters suggest that everything is working properly and that the system is not in any immediate danger. Vital signs outside normal parameters can signal trouble. Maybe a single component in the complex system is failing.

Organizations, like the human body, are extremely complex systems. They are composed of subsystems, which in turn, are composed of other sub-subsystems. In a complex system, subsystems tend to specialize. Some perform certain functions, while some do other things. Some, like the brain or heart, are absolutely critical for life, while others may be less important. Regardless of its purpose, however, each and every part of a system interacts with another part. In a healthy system, whether organizational or human, everything works together in a symbiotic or harmonious manner.

Monitor the Health of Your Organization

Benedict identified subordinate grumbling as the vital sign that he believed best indicated the health of an organizational system. Benedict actually used several different Latin words to express these signs of discontent, but his favorite was *murmurare*. This translates as "to make noise at a low volume"; in other words, to mutter or grumble. Complaining is probably too strong a translation. According to the Rule, these low tones of dissatisfaction need to be monitored and analyzed by the successful leader.

Vital signs are not just monitoring devices. Often vital signs that presage problems can develop a nasty life of their own. Left unchecked to fester and develop, a slight temperature can turn into a high fever that can destroy brain cells. Untreated, signs of problems can quickly kill the overall system.

This is how Benedict saw grumbling in the ranks. While it may be a valuable clue that something is wrong and that the organizational system is somehow out of harmony, grumbling itself can also destroy. If left untreated, grumbling can evolve into loud complaining and open rebellion. It can alter the harmony of the organization and attack the essence of group cohesion as quickly as a high fever can damage a human body. To Benedict, if the leader monitors and manages only one organizational vital sign, it should be subordinate grumbling. Tracking grumbling should be an obsession for the senior executive, not for punitive reasons but as a way of keeping a finger on the pulse of organizational health.

Benedict's emphasis on grumbling is seen by how frequently the Rule mentions it. Grumbling or muttering is discussed in several different chapters. The Rule tells subordinates to "not grumble or speak ill of others." (Rule, 4) Benedict notes that subordinate obedience, if done while grumbling, is still not true obedience. (Rule, 5) The Rule states, "First and foremost, there must be no word or sign of the evil of grumbling, no manifestation of it for any reason at all." (Rule, 34) Benedict requires discipline for those who "grumble," (Rule, 23) and in referring to subordinates, Benedict writes, "Above all else we admonish them to refrain from grumbling." (Rule, 40)

Benedict is quick to note that a leader's decisions may be the root cause for subordinate grumbling. There may be perfectly legitimate reasons for subordinates to mutter and grouse. For example, the Rule warns: "Similarly [the leader] should so regulate and arrange all matters [so that] the brothers may go about their activities without justifiable grumbling," (Rule, 41) and makes it clear that the leader is responsible for allocating work fairly so that subordinates can "perform their services without grumbling." (Rule, 53)

The Lessons of Grumbling

Benedict's many references to subordinate grumbling provides several lessons for the leader:

First, subordinate grumbling will effectively destroy the basis of group cohesion; it undermines the respect that bonds the community together. But unlike overt subordinate disobedience, grumbling is subtle; it often goes unnoticed by the senior leaders until too late.

Second, grumbling is contagious, and if left untreated it can take on a life of its own. Like a malignant cancer, a culture of grumbling can rapidly spread to attack the most remote corners of an organization.

Third, some people may just be chronic grumblers and habitual whiners. But Benedict sees a clear and present danger in such behavior. Discontent, if expressed publicly within an otherwise cohesive community, will inevitably become a focal point of more serious systemic illness in the future. To Benedict, die-hard grumblers must be identified, and the lessons of the Rule subsequently applied to hopefully improve such behaviors.

Fourth, poor management decisions can cause grumbling by even the most dedicated employee. Grumbling may, in fact, be "justified," to use the Rule's language. Grumbling can always be an indication of systemic illness, something that will need deeper investigation.

To Benedict, the root cause of grumbling must always be identified. Whether caused by a poor management decision or the errant attitudes of one individual, the effective leader, once aware of grumbling, needs to give it immediate and careful attention. Like all vital signs, grumbling, discontent, and negative comments may not be specific enough to pinpoint the exact problem—but they do raise early warning signals and important red flags.

Pay Attention to Your Public Face

Hospitality is infectious; it provides a first impression of corporate goodwill and permeates the organization with its contagious optimism. The Rule specifies that a certain type of person should staff the so-called "front desk," someone who is informed and hospitable. This is the point of first contact for all those coming in contact with an organization. To Benedict, this point of first contact required special attention. It is where potential customers get their first opportunity to interact with the organization and where lasting impressions are created. Goodwill can be built or destroyed at the front door of a business.

Effective modern leaders, such as Walt Disney, have practiced this lesson with great results. Disney knew that parking attendants, ticket sellers, and custodians—not the Mickey Mouse characters—provided the first impressions of Disneyland to customers. A grumpy parking lot attendant can snatch the magic away from the Magic Kingdom before the very first ride. Disney made sure that special attention, training, and rewards were given to these seemingly unglamorous positions.

Leadership the Benedictine Way

- Grumbling is the most important vital sign of group health and dysfunction.
- Grumbling needs to be tracked and the source of the grumbling needs to be identified.
- Grumbling is contagious and infectious.
- Some grumbling may, in fact, be justified; if so, fix the problem.

III
the rule of empowerment

lessons for honing
your self

13

The ᚱᚢᛚᛖ of Leader Example:
Delisting the Corporate Coward

Anyone who receives the name of [the leader] is to lead his disciples by a twofold teaching: He must point out to them all that is good . . . more by example than by words.

—The Rule of St. Benedict (Rule, 2)

o Benedict, one simply could not be an effective leader except by example. He had studied the leadership principles of successful organizations during the zenith of Greco-Roman power and had personally seen the leadership failures of the now weak Roman Empire that was collapsing around him.

Benedict had reflected on his expanding network of monasteries and schools, and the successes and failures of his own personal leadership during this time. Everywhere he turned, Benedict always reached the same conclusion—great leaders lead by example. This principle of walking the walk is referenced throughout the Rule: "Anyone who receives the name of [the leader] is to lead his disciples by a twofold teaching: He must point out to them all that is good . . . more by example than by words." Benedict repeats this warning: "Again, if the leader teaches his disciples that something is not to be done, then neither must he do it." (Rule, 2)

Many people preach leadership but then fail to heed their own advice. Everything we know about Benedict's personal life suggests that he stood above all in following his own Rule. The source for most of our information about Benedict comes from the writings of Pope Gregory I of Rome (540–604). As Gregory notes in *The Second Book of Dialogues* (translated into English by P. W. and printed at Paris in 1608; re-edited by Edmund G.

Gardner in 1911; and again by the Saint Pachomius Library in 1995), Benedict "wrote a rule for his monks, both excellent for discretion and also eloquent for the style. Of whose life and conversation, if any be curious to know further, he may in the institution of that rule understand all his manner of life and discipline: for Benedict could not otherwise teach, than himself lived." (Gregory, 36)

Benedict rose in the morning before his monks, (Gregory, 35) stayed and prayed longer than his disciples, (Gregory, 29) worked long hours with his monks in the fields, (Gregory, 32) and regularly put himself at personal risk, such as once negotiating with a murderer for the release of a hostage. (Gregory, 31)

Watch Out for the Corporate Coward

When we think of the great stories of courage, we usually think of those involving leadership by example. Lord Cardigan was at the front of the Light Brigade as it charged into the valley of death during the Crimean War. Lord Nelson stood in full uniform on the deck of the HMS *Victory*, more exposed than any of his sailors during the battle of Trafalgar.

Unfortunately, it seems as if the practice of leadership by example is in decline. More and more, the rule of "do as I tell you, not as I do" appears to be the norm. The modern world appears to be institutionalizing the perception of organizational cowardice, a sense that leaders have carefully and methodically insulated themselves from the rigorous demands of leadership by example.

One is reminded of L. Frank Baum's wonderful book *Ozma of Oz,* the 1908 sequel to *The Wizard of Oz.* Queen Ozma's army numbered twenty-seven: Eight generals, seven colonels, six majors, five captains all dressed in the finest uniforms and medals, and one insignificant poor private. When finally ordered into battle, the once flamboyant and seemingly brave commanding general immediately changed his demeanor. He nervously said to Ozma, "'I and my brother officers all suffer from heart disease, and the slightest excitement might kill us . . . Private soldiers are not, I believe, afflicted that way.' Thus the general ordered the attack. 'For-ward-march' cried all the generals with one voice. 'For-ward-march' yelled the colonels. 'For-ward-march' shouted the majors. 'For-ward-march' commanded the captains. And at that the private leveled his spear and dashed furiously upon the foe."[1] At modern corporations, many chief executive officers—those with more modern medals and perks—work fewer hours and receive large raises, even when their companies are on the verge of bankruptcy. Most college administrators could not survive the rigorous tenure process they demand of their professors. In the modern army, generals will never be put in harm's way; in fact, today they are ordered by their fellow generals to stay safely hidden in the rear. The perception of managerial cowardice has, indeed, been institutionalized in many modern organizations. It seems as if only the lone private charges bravely forward.

Follow the Rule and Motivate by Example— No Exceptions

The rule of leadership by example sounds almost trivial, but for some reason the lesson just does not seem to stick.

According to management researchers, not setting a good example is the most common complaint that people have about their bosses. Yet throughout history, senior executives have offered every possible apology and excuse for their behaviors. But the Benedictine system of leadership does not allow exceptions to this principle. Arguments for executive privilege ring hollow for Benedict. Justifications of "I deserve it now, I paid my dues" fall well short of the Rule's voice. Apologies of "my leadership talent is too important to risk my time, life, or limb in the trenches" won't be found in Benedict's vocabulary.

Many years ago, one of the authors spent several weeks living in a Benedictine monastery in central California. One of the most powerful images from this visit was a diary that the senior abbot kept. At the end of each day, the abbot wrote down and meditated on the personal examples he set for his monks. He noted his failures, and set a daily plan for improvement. He was not about to make excuses; he was just trying to follow Benedict's example.

The Benedictine leadership system recognizes that subordinates are motivated by two equal forces. The first force is the Rule, the well understood and consistent prescriptions for proper behavior. The second force is example. To Benedict, they are not only equal in motivational power, but must always be used together. To Benedict, leadership by example is an absolute virtue and one of the basic foundations of superior leadership. As the Rule states, "A [subordinate] does only what is endorsed by the common rule . . . as the example set by his superiors." (Rule, 7)

Leadership—Southern Style

Leadership in the American South has a distinctive style. The South is full of unassuming leaders who have built powerful corporations and amassed personal fortunes. Some are educated in the grand style of the Southern gentleman, while others are just good-old-boy entrepreneurs, drawn from the same mold as Wal-Mart's Sam Walton.

While most of our (the authors') professional lives have been spent in the high technology world of California, during the last ten years we have spent a great deal of time in the American South. We made a special effort to seek out and interview many of the great Southern leaders and entrepreneurs. We wanted to know their secrets of success. Above all, one theme has come out loud and clear—concentrate on the core values of leadership.

In a slow Southern drawl, one executive, a former attorney said, "I simply can't remember 200 leadership hints, but I am smart enough to remember the ten or fifteen most important and work from there." Another Southern entrepreneur we interviewed told a classic rags to riches story. Bill had made a fortune in the furniture trucking industry, and at eighty-three had finally retired to an oceanfront home in North Carolina, to fish and walk on the beach. His secret to leadership? "Only three principles," he said. "First, never go into debt [he paid cash for his beach home]. Second, always manage your employees like a stern but caring Southern father. And third, show your employees daily what you are made of—I get to work before the first employee and leave after the last clocks out. I don't need to tell my employees how hard I work; they can see it for themselves every day at work."

Leadership the Benedictine Way

- Subordinates do not listen to words when they are not accompanied by example.
- There are no exceptions to leadership by example.
- Keep track of your leadership examples, and study their failures and successes.

14

The ʀuʟe of Humility and Moderation: Turning Managerial Ego on Its Head

Whoever exalts himself shall be humbled and whoever humbles himself shall be exalted.

—The Rule of St. Benedict (Rule, 7)

history is littered with the bodies of egotistical leaders. From Napoleon at Waterloo to Custer at the Little Bighorn, it is vanity that clouds judgment and creates the conditions for crushing defeats. Benedict catalogued "excitability, anxiousness, extremism, pride, jealously and overly suspicious behavior" as important warning signs of poor leaders. (Rule, 64) He warned that individuals demonstrating such personality traits should never be placed in positions of authority.

To the early Christian church, humility was an important personal virtue, for leader and follower alike. Humility was grounded in the basic tenets of Christianity but, according to Benedict, was also a key component of sustainable organizational life.

Humility was so important to Benedict that he devoted one full chapter (Chapter 7) in the Rule to the topic. Other great spiritual writers of the time also stressed the fundamental importance of this virtue. As Augustine of Hippo (354–430) wrote: "Should you ask me, 'What is the first thing in a virtuous life?' I should reply, the first, second, and third thing therein— nay, all is humility." Likewise, the Greek archbishop John Chrysostom (347–407) noted, "Humility is the root, mother, nurse, foundation, and bond of all virtue." To these writers, humility does not mean timidity or a broken spirit. Compassion must be carefully distinguished from a groveling attitude—Benedict is quite clear on this. Humility, in its purest form, is actually the greatest source of personal power.

To some readers, the notion of humility as a necessary tenet of leadership may seem in conflict with our modern world where pride, self-promotion, and assertiveness are often taught and valued as important leadership traits. But the ancient Roman world in which Benedict lived was also immersed in pride, ego, and self-promotion. Essentially unregulated, leadership and power were often realized by the blade of a sword, overt bribes of gold, or energetic and gaudy displays of wealth and power.

Benedict was born of a noble family. As a young man he had servants, was surrounded by money and privilege, and was groomed for a job in the Roman bureaucracy. Yet he still came to passionately believe that humility, above all other marks of character, was the key to true leadership. For the follower, worker, and employee, humility is reflected in a call for obedience to authority. As Benedict notes, "The first step of humility is obedience . . . with the ready step of obedience, they follow the voice of authority in their actions." (Rule, 5)

The Rule stresses that humility is particularly important for those in positions of leadership. While, for the employee on a lower rung, humility is reflected in obedience, and taking instructions; for the leader or senior executive, humility must be reflected in discretion, compassion, and moderation in action and command. These are the outward traits of true humility, the tangible executive behaviors subordinates should see every day.

The Rule is full of such warnings to would-be leaders: "Whoever exalts himself shall be humbled and whoever humbles himself shall be exalted" (Rule, 7), and in a later chapter, "Excitable, anxious, extreme, obstinate, jealous or over suspicious [the leader] must not be. Such a man is never at rest. Instead he must show forethought and consideration in his orders. . . . He should be discerning and moderate." (Rule, 64)

Robert E. Lee on Humility

Confederate General Robert E. Lee is often cited as the epitome of leadership by humility. General Lee had a particular presence around his troops. His men, from the lowest private to the most senior officers, gave their unwavering devotion to him. Lee's command over his armies was unsurpassed. Lee's secret was his deep humility. He was never boisterous or proud. He spoke only in quiet tones, with care and kindness. He gave credit to others for his magnificent victories, but took immediate responsibility even in his rare defeat.

According to the magazine *Military History,* Robert E. Lee was the "model American general embodying traits of devotion, humility and self-sacrifice." While the pompous Union general, George McClellan, strutted in and out of Washington dinner parties, the outnumbered Lee methodically rode circles around the Union army. Lincoln finally had to fire McClellan.

What was Robert E. Lee's source of humility? Lee did not mince words on this aspect of leadership: It was his faith. He read and studied the great spiritual leaders of Christianity. As it was to Benedict and the other great monastic leaders, to Robert E. Lee humility and faith became intertwined. To these great leaders, humility becomes part of their daily lives. As H. W.

Crocker, author of the book *Robert E. Lee on Leadership* (Rocklin, Calif.: Forum, 1999), notes, Lee "won field command through that neglected Christian virtue—humility."

Learn Humility Early

The lessons of humility must be learned early in a management career. Benedict suggested watching even the most junior of managers. For example, he gave his middle managers the admonishment: "If perhaps one of these deans is found to be puffed up with any pride, and so deserving of censure, he is to be reproved." (Rule, 21) Elsewhere he added: "Therefore, drawing on this and other examples of discretion [moderation], the mother of virtues, [the leader] must arrange everything so that the strong have something to yearn for and the weak nothing to run from." (Rule, 64)

Power is dangerous without the check of humility. In business, leaders can make or break the careers of their employees. In universities, they can pass or fail struggling students. In armies, they can send young men and women to their death. To Benedict, authority must always be balanced by personal humility; the more authority a leader has, the more he or she needs true humility. Power, combined with pride, greed, and arrogance, however, is a sure prescription for failure.

It is no accident that the formal title "abbot," the supreme leader of a Benedictine community, comes from the Aramaic word *abba*, meaning "father". Benedict realized that if leaders are to expect obedience they must, in turn, show compassion, moderation, kindness, and care. The leader, Benedict wrote, should "avoid extremes, otherwise by rubbing too hard to remove the rust, [the leader] may break the vessel." Benedict continues by exhorting the leader to "recognize his goal must be profit for the [subordinates], not preeminence for himself." (Rule, 64)

Sources of Pride

Pride has many faces, and they all must be properly harnessed. The great medieval abbot and theologian Bernard of Clairvaux (1090–1153) discussed twelve sources of pride in his book, *Steps of Humility and Pride*. Here are just five important types of pride:

1. *The pride of natural ego.* We all like to see our reflection. At your house, do you have a framed picture of just yourself, with nobody else in the picture?

2. *The pride of achievement.* The pride that arises from accomplishment. Do you enjoy telling people what you have done, or do you have trophies and awards on display where other people can see them?

3. *The pride of association.* The pride that arises from association with more powerful people or organizations. Do you attend parties or choose your friends based upon their status or power?

4. *The pride of power.* Pride can arise from power over people and money. Do you hire people that you know are not as smart as you, and therefore don't present a threat?

5. *The pride of emotion.* Emotions can also create powerful images of pride. Do you think you are special because you are in love, have a family, or look attractive?

While such examples of pride may be natural human traits that need little encouragement, humility certainly does not come as naturally. After all, most of the animal world struts and puffs to show its superiority. Humility must be cultivated and nurtured. While some modern leadership writers recognize humility as a trait of good leadership, they all stop short of teaching us how to acquire this skill. How can we learn true humility?

Fortunately there is a body of work that can help: the amazing writings and lives of the Christian mystics. Their exercises in acquiring true humility, such as those written by Ignatius of Loyola (1491–1556) in his *Spiritual Exercises,* are rooted in 2,000 years of practice. Humility, these great mystics cautioned, must be carefully acquired. Like studying math, music, and reading, learning humility is an ascending path of knowledge. It simply takes time and practice.

Benedict's Steps to Humility

In the Rule, Benedict defines twelve progressive steps on the ladder to learning true humility. In modern terms, they are:

Step 1: *Revere the simple rules.* Start by following simple rules: Don't speed, stop at red lights, meet deadlines.
Step 2: *Reject your personal desires.* Consciously temper your

basic desires, fast when a little hungry, avoid impulse buying, skip dessert after dinner.

Step 3: *Obey others.* Willingly and without any internal grumbling obey others in positions of authority.

Step 4: *Endure affliction.* Consciously turn the other cheek when upset, even if you are in the right.

Step 5: *Confess your weaknesses.* Regularly acknowledge, even to just yourself, your failings. Spell out the details.

Step 6: *Practice contentment.* Try to be content with your job, status in life, and the old car.

Step 7: *Learn self reproach.* Develop a conscious effort to see yourself as humble and truly lucky to have whatever you have in life. This requires serious internal reflection.

Step 8: *Obey the common rule.* Obey all the organizational rules, not just in letter, but also in spirit. In particular, follow the Rule of Benedict.

Step 9: *Understand that silence is golden.* Consciously try to listen more than speak. Don't give as many executive orders.

Step 10: *Meditate on humility.* Meditate on the seriousness of humility, and let this seriousness enter into your actions and speech.

Step 11: *Speak simply.* Talk in a low voice, speak gently, and with kindness to everyone.

Step 12: *Act humble in appearance.* Be humble in appearance as well as in the heart. Tone down the expensive dress and elegant tastes.

Benedict reminds us to study these steps but above all to practice them in everyday life. The Rule recognizes that executive humility is a complex emotion. True humility is learned by attempting the first step—reverence to simple rules—then moving progressively higher with practice. A child does not start with advanced calculus until learning simple addition and subtraction. From a thousand years of practice, the mystics all have the same advice—slow down. Don't take a higher step until you master an earlier one. Just as in practicing the piano, what starts as a tedious exercise soon becomes a musical masterpiece. To Benedict, this is the path to executive humility.

Beware of False Humility

Be careful of false humility. C. S. Lewis in the *Screwtape Letters* noted this problem: "Catch a man at the moment when he is really poor in spirit and smuggle into his mind the gratifying reflection, 'by jove! I'm being humble,' and almost immediately pride at his own humility will appear."

It is no accident that Benedict put "appearances" as the twelfth step. His attitude is that one must act like a monk before looking like a monk. In fact, this is Benedict's opinion about acquiring all noble virtues—before dressing for the part, learn how to play the part. Looking humble has become quite fashionable in some circles today. While recently dining with a large group in a rather upscale restaurant in La Jolla, California one of the authors enjoyed listening to two affluent young couples in their thirties intently debating how to dress humble, but still appear wealthy. They agreed that the blue jeans had to look faded, but not too ragged and the oversized sweaters shouldn't hide the Cartier watches and gold bangles. They had obviously skipped the first eleven steps in Benedict's ladder of humility and gone straight to the twelfth. Benedict is clear, however, that true humility comes from having "climbed *all* these steps of humility." (Rule, 7)

Leadership the Benedictine Way

- The basic leadership virtue is the rule of humility.
- A leader's actions must always contain the seeds of humility.
- Humility is reflected by decisions of discretion, compassion, kindness, care, and moderation.
- Signs of pride must be thoughtfully rejected.
- True humility is a learned skill that comes from exercise and training.

15

The RULE of Iron Resolve: Taming the Inner Bulldog

First of all, every time you begin a good work, you must . . . bring it to perfection.

> —The Rule of St. Benedict (Rule, prologue)

he second of Benedict's great personal leadership virtues is fortitude and inner strength. At several points in the Rule, he emphasizes these positive traits. For example, he praises the Christian hermits of the day for their incredible resolve. He writes, "They have built up their strength and go from the battle line in the ranks of their brothers to the single combat of the desert. Self-reliant now, without the support of another, they are ready with God's help to grapple single-handed with the vices of body and mind." (Rule, 2)

The military metaphor is not lost on readers of the Rule. It takes strength, willpower, and a dogged determination to be a monk. Benedict values such virtues, whether in the lone Christian hermit or within the organizational boundaries of a monastery. He asks that whoever starts an activity should always try "to bring it to perfection." (Rule, prologue) Productive work is not an easy task, but one that takes fortitude and strength. And it is even tougher for the executive who must stand above all others in this effort. According to Benedict, "Let the leader understand also what a difficult and arduous task [he or she] has undertaken." (Rule, 2)

Benedict and his followers throughout the ages demonstrated nothing short of amazing stamina and entrepreneurial spirit. They initiated new organizations and expanded old organizations. They adapted to changing circumstances and developed new ways of competing in a difficult world. They had a passionate resolve that would embarrass the toughest bulldog. For hundreds of years they were the world's foremost explorers and innovators. They built monasteries on the roughest mountains, brought the light of reason to the depth of the Dark Ages, and withstood the cruelest slaughter and torture throughout the centuries. Yet they always persevered.

Combine Bulldog Resolve with Executive Humility

But Benedict also knew that willpower, passion, and resolve needed to be tempered and directed. He makes this point when he writes, "If a brother is requested to do something difficult or impossible he should, at first, accept the command meekly and obediently." (Rule, 68) This is a powerful Benedictine theme, and like a chapel bell it rings time and time again in the Rule. A good leader (and subordinate) must have an unmatched bulldog resolve and gritty determination. They must "toil faithfully at all of these tasks." (Rule, 4)

But this determination must be properly controlled within the Benedictine framework of humility and obedience; it has to work within the Rule. Benedict purposely thrusts the executive into the heart of an apparent paradox, a battle of furious opposites. On one hand, the leader's effort must be determined and strenuous. Benedict asks the executive to be entrepreneurial and venturous. Not only that, he demands that the leader encourage his subordinates to push themselves to the absolute limit. On the other hand, he recognizes that both the source and the ultimate control of this inner strength arise from the virtues of humility and obedience. This is the foundation for the Benedictine leadership system—work the paradox between bulldog resolve and monastic humility.

In the mind of any Benedictine monk, personal humility and personal resolve must be held in absolute harmony; they must work synergistically. The life of a Benedictine monk requires it. And the executive must live at the pinnacle of this paradox.

Resolve and Humility Are Universal

Management researcher and author Jim Collins studied eleven great companies over fifteen years, and concluded that the key to leadership is personal humility combined with personal will. His often-quoted *Harvard Business Review* article "Level 5 Leadership" (January 2001) on transformational leadership appears to be a study in contrasts. "Modest and willful, shy and fearless, humility and drive" are Collins's observations of excellent leaders. To use Collins's model, these leaders have reached Level 5 Leadership. This is not a new idea, however. Level 5 Leadership sounds a lot like Benedictine Leadership.

To Benedict, humility and moderation does not diminish the entrepreneurial spirit and willpower; it simply redirects it. This is the point of the Benedictine leadership system—honest and true humility channels the most powerful natural passion to excel. True entrepreneurship and leadership resolve does not come from the pride and ego, but rather from the personal passion to excel, to improve both the organization and the world around it. It is this well-directed passion within that drives the entrepreneurial spirit, and that paved the way for the amazing diversity and success of Benedictine institutions. For Benedict, these are the starting and end points for superior leadership.

Managing Outside the Box

To Benedict, great leadership involves interacting with subordinates at a one-on-one level on a regular basis. This type of personal leadership requires a basic knowledge of each and every person who is within the managerial sphere.

Benedict recommended a personal leadership style that is flexible and varies with the circumstances. Within the strict boundaries of the Rule and its ethics, Benedict noted that a superior leader should be "by turns, stern as a taskmaster, devoted and tender as only a father can be. With the undisciplined and restless, he will use firm argument; with the obedient and docile and patient, he will appeal for greater virtue; but as for the negligent and disdainful, we charge him to use reproof and rebuke." (Rule, 2)

This is a recurring Benedictine theme: Keep your eye on the basic principles of leadership and the clear path of ethical behavior, but also feel free to improvise as the situation merits or the personalities of the subordinates change.

Leadership the Benedictine Way

- Aim high, but with a bowed head.
- Recognize the leadership paradox of bulldog resolve and executive humility.
- True entrepreneurial passion arises from the desire to improve, not from individual pride and ego.

Final Thoughts: Playing the Core Melody

In this book we have tried to present the top-of-the-mind issues covered by the Rule of St. Benedict, those ideas that form the crux of the Benedictine leadership and management model. Combined, they constitute the timeless core melody for superior managerial improvisation.

Clearly, after fifteen centuries of organizational history, all types of problems, from annoying daily frustrations to deadly crises, have been hotly debated within the walls of Benedictine monasteries, and ultimately tested against the legislation of the Rule. Benedict attempted to cover many things, but most of all he tried to present a clear and coherent picture of sustainable organization and superior leadership. Without question, his Rule represents one of the earliest and most complete self-contained systems of management.

Does it work? Yes. At least this is the overwhelming evidence from fifteen centuries of organizations that have been guided by nothing more than a copy of Benedict's Rule and the managerial improvisation of individual executives and abbots that fill in the Rule's edges with modern relevance.

Many authors suggest Benedict was born fifteen centuries too early. They believe that Benedict was really a modern thinker stuck in an ancient time. We see it in a different light. Benedict, we argue, was born at exactly the right time. He lived during one of the most critical crossroads of history and at a time when genius truly set the stage for future generations. Benedict was close enough to the pinnacle of Greco-Roman thought and culture to study its incredible successes, but also lived through its failures and witnessed its ultimate collapse. Benedict was part of the early Christian movement that concentrated on the fundamental principles of life and being, without being caught up in the nuances of later scholarly debates. He was privy to the oral traditions and the (now mostly lost) writings of previous monastic leaders, but he also arrived at a point in time when no one had yet pulled it all together. Above all, he was a keen observer of human nature, a genius of synthesis and summation, and a charismatic leader.

Without Benedict, the Western world would have certainly gone in a different direction. What direction that would have been one can only speculate. Without question, however, Benedict did illuminate an important part of the long and treacherous path leading to the modern world. He was, in our opinion, the first real modern leadership thinker. Best of all, he wrote his ideas down.

Michel Foucault, the famous French historian of human sciences, argues that modernity is born from a "shock of ideas," a point in time when there are episodic periods of social and theoretical rupture. Early sixth-century Rome was at this intersection, and Benedict was at the forefront. Benedict created the contextual pattern for much of the discussion on organization and leadership of later centuries, a healthy debate that continues to this very day.

Benedict, as did many of the early Christian thinkers of the day, saw the human condition as a pattern of rhythmic waves, something that flowed and ebbed between time and nature. He believed it was the leader's primary job to harmonize these various cycles of physical labor, intellectual development, and human satisfaction into a cohesive, productive, and sustainable organization. His Rule is written in this spirit.

Writers of historical books will always wonder if the person they were writing about would agree with the basic points of the book. In writing this book we have tried to assume Benedict was looking over our shoulders; whenever a loud "humph" was heard, we would back up, regroup our thoughts, and rewrite again. We hope that Benedict would agree with our effort.

Without question, Benedict would most certainly want to expand material in one particular area, the notion of spirituality in organizations. To Benedictines, work has an important and clear spiritual meaning; it is something to be deeply valued. Effective leaders can enhance the nature of work, and by this power, have a spiritual obligation. Benedict, no doubt, would want this concept developed further.

We, too, agree with this. As we stated from the very beginning, however, this book is meant as a discussion of leadership and management, not as a treatise of theology. Thus, we have purposely focused on issues of leadership, organization, and management, and attempted to present them in a somewhat neutral way for a cross section of readers. A basic premise of this book is that history is an incredible repository of leadership thought and professional experimentation, yet it is rarely tapped by modern writers and practitioners. Aristotle (384–322 B.C.), for example, developed important theorems about justice and commercial exchange that apply today. Augustine (343–430) upgraded the moral value of work to its modern levels while Benedict (480–547) provided the framework for modern leadership principles.

Friar Pierre Jean d'Olieu (1248–1298) was probably the father of modern entrepreneurial economic theory, forcibly arguing for the moral and economic contributions of the entrepreneurial class. And the late-sixteenth-century economic theologians of the Spanish School of Salamanca made significant arguments about the liberalization of international markets, and that the market mechanism was the most efficient allocator of resources that predated the more well-known economist Adam Smith by two centuries.

Throughout the ages, writers such as these have always meticulously studied and carefully expanded the lessons of history. They know what the great thinkers of previous centuries have added to the paradigm, and they know what has been discarded and why. Useful leadership thought and practice is not created in a vacuum. Expounding on these important issues without accessing the immense reservoir of organizational history and literature is only a recent, and perhaps somewhat dangerous, phenomenon. This trend is particularly evident among the plethora of "experientially" based leadership and management books currently found in bookstores. It seems as if anyone who has managed a firm, raised venture capital, hired an employee, or destroyed a dot.com business writes a book about the experience.

We do not expect that upon reading this short book a modern CEO would change his or her formal corporate title to Chief Abbot, insist all the company's employees address each other as "brother" or "sister," or have a communal singing of the fifty-first Psalm each workday by the coffee machine. This should not happen anymore than an army general, upon first completing Sun Tzu's *Art of War,* would retire his armored division of Abram tanks and replace them with a phalanx of archers and spear throwers. This completely misses the point of the book.

We believe the Rule provides the most basic and essential ingredients for creating a truly sustainable organization, whether in the corporate world or public sector. But like an award-winning pastry, the finest ingredients must still be added with care, combined and stirred with proper technique, then appropriately baked with the attention and diligence of a master's eye. This is the art of cooking, and the art of leadership and management as well. Even with the most solid of foundations, it still requires skill and subtle improvisation, appropriate to the time and place to make a truly superior organization.

We sincerely hope that our book about Benedict of Nursia and his leadership model is viewed within this context.

Appendix I

The Seeds of Modern Leadership Theory

The first 200 years of Christianity was a time of passionate belief and violent uncertainty. Under the constant threat of state persecution, groups of like-minded individuals would often band together into small, autonomous religious communities, often located some distance from the population centers of the day.[1] Here, somewhat isolated from the distractions of daily urban life and the soldiers of Rome, people sought a spiritual bonding surrounded by their fellow believers. Over time, dozens of these isolated rural Christian communities began to take root and flourish throughout the Mediterranean.

As these small communities took root and expanded, the matter of proper governance became an important issue. Daily life needed to be managed: Livestock needed tending, children required care, and houses had to be erected. People from the entire spectrum of society, from former slaves and courtesans to noble sons and daughters, had to live and work together, oftentimes under the harshest of conditions.

The early Church Fathers could not provide much direction or guidance to these remote congregations. In addition to the threat of state arrest and possible execution, these harried leaders were preoccupied with establishing the theological tenets of a new faith. Instituting a formal Church hierarchy to regulate remote spiritual communities was simply not a priority. The method and form of governance had to be worked out by trial and error, internally by the community itself without any outside help.

Given the basic egalitarian principles of Christianity, democratic rule soon became the standard of governance for these early communities. An elected leader or council typically governed, but there was little organizational stability. Members of the community came and went as they pleased, often migrating between different religious bands. For that time in history, these early Christian communities were truly a unique experiment in organization. Autonomous by necessity, fiercely independent by choice, and staunchly democratic, these small bands of Christians were to become one of the focal points for the future development of monastic orders throughout the world.

Another focal point was the Christian hermit, the ascetic who sought spiritual perfection and mystical bliss by accepting vows of celibacy and poverty and living in isolation. These reclusive hermits lived alone on the fringes of Christian communities. They found solitude in nearby caves and empty tombs, in the mud huts of the Egyptian desert, and atop rugged mountain peaks.

Though hermits were, by and large, almost completely isolated, there was some economic and interpersonal interaction with the local Christian congregation. The charity of the nearby communities sustained the hermits, and they in turn would repay the debt by giving spiritual advice and insight.

The Birth of the Modern Organization

From these two powerful traditions, the importance of community and the need for individual fulfillment, emerged a structure for the monastic system that continues to this day. By the end of the third century, a fusion of community life and ascetic idealism was taking place. The dominant organizational view was one that combined the active life of social support and interaction with the importance of deep contemplation and the individual pursuit of spiritual happiness.

Thus, the concept of community interest was successfully merged with the need for personal fulfillment. For the first time in history, on a large scale there was a clear recognition that the individual's needs, desires, and interests had to be carefully and explicitly considered in the design and management of effective organizations.

The monastic concept was beginning to form. Single men started to separate from the broader religious congregations and form their own private communities with the more ascetic vows of celibacy and poverty. Likewise, single women banded together, typically on the other side of some river or valley to minimize the obvious, more worldly temptations of the flesh. These communities of men and women often lived in symbiotic harmony, with men providing food and manual labor and women sewing clothes and baking bread.

As these communities of men and women formed, they promptly incorporated the important traditions of autonomy and democratic governance of the broader Christian congregations. Men elected their leaders, the abbots, while women elected theirs, the prioresses. But they also fought to maintain the ideals of individual fulfillment so firmly grounded in the tradition of the honored mystics of the caves and deserts.

Over time the Roman state became more tolerant. It became easier for Christians to openly live in the outside world, to conduct business and participate in all levels of society. Finally, when emperor Constantine the Great promised protection with the Edict of Milan in A.D. 313, the last real reason for families and others not inclined to the monastic life was removed. Only the small, remote communities of men and women dedicated to this combination of community life and spiritual contemplation remained.

Balance the Individual and the Organization

While it was not until Benedict that the full monastic tradition coalesced into the form that carried it into modern times, the writings of Basil the Great (329–379), Gregory of Nyssa (332–394), Augustine of Hippo (354–430), and John Cassian (360–435) all expanded the notion of community in several important directions, particularly as the Western and Eastern churches started to move apart.

Common to all of these monastic writings was the blending of organizational imperative with individual interests. Not only did the community's success depend upon the satisfaction of each and every member's interests, but the individual needed the team in order to prosper on a personal level.

Unlike the Roman leadership practice of the day, which was preoccupied with the interests of the ruling classes, the monastic system was sensitive to the needs of all individuals. It no longer had bearing whether or not the individual was a former slave or born to title and rank; every individual, whatever his or her station in society, had inherent worth. Thus, the concept of organization radically shifted, and leadership theory was forever altered.

It was this emerging, more modern view of organizations that became the basis for Benedict's Rule. Now, organizations needed to enhance the abilities of the individual in addition to achieving a common objective. Under the Rule, the Three Musketeers' call of "all for one and one for all" finally began to have real meaning.

Appendix II

Benedictine Contributions to World Culture

For a variety of reasons the contributions of the Christian monastic orders to both the preservation of ancient knowledge and the development of modern institutions has been largely ignored. In part, this is due to a mistaken association between the monastic orders and the Dark Ages. In fact, the monastic orders were largely responsible for carrying the beacon of light and knowledge during these difficult times.

The so-called Dark Ages of A.D. 400 to 800 were indeed a period of uncertainty, strife, and confusion. By the fifth century, Roman control over much of Europe simply evaporated, to be replaced by the local tribal systems and primitive cultures.

The faith of Christianity was just beginning to make its first inroads into Europe, including the British Isles and Ireland. During this time, the Benedictine monks and sisters were at the forefront of missionary work, slowly establishing networks of small monasteries for men and women. These small, poor monasteries, surviving under the harshest of conditions, became the true islands of learning, agriculture, medicine, and historical preservation. It was not until the Carolingian Empire and the reign of Charlemagne in the ninth and tenth centuries that most, but certainly not all, of Europe ceded to Christianity,

 143

and the monasteries had a degree of protection and safety.

Working in these islands of knowledge, Benedictines made important contributions in many areas of world development.

Contribution to Agriculture

Over the centuries, the Benedictines developed many modern concepts of agriculture. Most often their monasteries were sited in remote and inhospitable locations, on land that was previously thought unsuitable for farming. Out of necessity, these monastic communities developed or dramatically improved sophisticated agricultural systems such as terracing, drainage, irrigation, crop rotation, and selective breeding in order to survive. Many of the Benedictines' techniques are still used today. According to French historian François Pierre Guillaume Guizot, "The Benedictine monks were the agriculturists of Europe."[1]

Contribution to Medicine and Hospitals

After the fall of Rome, one of the few places scholars could feel secure was within the walls of monasteries. It was here that records and books were kept in safety. The monastic orders kept alive the traditions of Roman medical theory for hundreds of years.

Outside the monasteries, the study of medicine and the institutionalized care of the sick essentially ceased, or reverted to primitive conditions, such as Druid- or Celtic-styled medicine. As the medical historian Dr. Mayeaux notes: "After the fall of the Roman Empire, some areas that were not under the control of the Christian Church returned to the more primitive forms of medicine. The Gallo-Celtic peoples used this system until the monks Christianized all of Europe and brought with them the Roman-style medicine."[2]

By contrast, Benedict's Rule provided for a specific location to care for the sick and needy, and a compassion and attentive "infirmarian" to run the medical complex. (Rule, 36) Monks kept pharmacies and provided free care to the sick of the surrounding community under Christian hospitality. The Rule became the foundation for the modern concept of hospitals.

The first true modern hospital is considered to be the Benedictine monastery of St. Gall in Switzerland. By the mid-700s it had a complete medical complex including a medical herb garden, specific rooms for the sick, a pharmacy, a medical library, separate lodging for physicians, and a specialized nursing staff.

Contribution to Education and Document Preservation

After the fall of Rome, several forces were at work. First, by Benedict's time, with the cycles of famine, invasion, and disease, many families were sending their children to monasteries for safekeeping. The Rule of Benedict specifically addressed the care and status of such children, so there should be little surprise that there evolved in monasteries the first large-scale egalitarian school system, one in which the child of a slave could be educated next to the child of a nobleman. Many of the great modern universities of Europe, such as Oxford, are built upon the physical and intellectual foundations of previous Benedictine colleges.

Second, Benedict required the reading of books by his monks. Out of this came another important monastic tradition, the support of libraries and the preservation of scholarship and literary art. Perhaps one of the greatest contributions of the monastic orders, particularly the Benedictines, was the collection, preservation, and dissemination of these literary works of antiquity, both secular and sacred.

As Heather Millar wrote in *The Electronic Scriptorium* (*www.wired.com/wired/archive/4.08/es.cybermonks.html*), "Aeschylus's great tragedy about Agamemnon and Cassandra; Euripides's romantic story of Jason and Medea; Plato's 'Necessity is mother of invention' and his ideas of soul and sin; the logic and scientific system of Aristotle; the penitent meditations of Marcus Aurelius Antoninus, the grandiose speeches of Cicero that have inspired politicians through the ages—none of these would have survived without the monastic scriptoria. The monks even saved the erotic works of Ovid and Sappho, by reading Christian sentiments into the steamy pagan poetry."

Contribution to the Hospitality Industry

One of the demands of the Rule is proper reception of guests, travelers, and pilgrims. Poor and rich, believer and nonbeliever are to be warmly welcomed. Benedict makes a point of expecting guests and travelers at his communities; he writes, for example, "The abbot's table must always be with guests and travelers." (Rule, 56)

But Benedict also set standards in the Rule for the monks' reception of such guests—the first universal code of hospitality. An entire chapter of the Rule is dedicated to this. Guests and travelers are to be properly greeted with the greatest hospitality, shown secure guest rooms, provided clean bedding, allowed to dine at the "captain's table," and warmly sent on their way.

From a hospitality point of view, the guest facilities at the monasteries emphasized cleanliness, security, and a warm, friendly, and impeccably honest staff. In a sense the Benedictines were the first large-scaled "franchise" hotel system in the world, and set many of the standards for today's concept of hospitality. The Benedictines provided the primary lodging facilities for travelers for almost 800 years, until around the thirteenth and fourteenth centuries when larger privately owned hotels under the control of an innkeeper guild began to appear.

Contribution to the International Banking System

In A.D. 1118 a group of knights under Hugh of Payens and Godfey of Saint-Omeror formed the "Poor Knights of Christ and of the Temple of Solomon," or the Knights Templar, the first of the military monastic orders of the Crusades. The Rule they adopted was based on the Rule of Benedict.

Over the following centuries, the Knights Templar grew in power, acquiring wealth and estates. One of their most noted contributions was in the area of banking. Essentially inventing the modern international banking system of deposits, loans, credits, and the various instruments of international finance, they financed most the European governments and royalty of the time.

Appendix III

Excerpts from the Rule

The following selections are taken from *The Holy Rule of Benedict*, 1949 edition. Translated by Rev. Boniface Verheyen, OSB of St. Benedict's Abbey, Atchison, Kansas. Used with permission.

PROLOGUE

Listen, O my son, to the precepts of thy master, and incline the ear of thy heart, and cheerfully receive and faithfully execute the admonitions of thy loving Father, that by the toil of obedience thou mayest return to Him from whom by the sloth of disobedience thou hast gone away.

To thee, therefore, my speech is now directed, who, giving up thine own will, takest up the strong and most excellent arms of obedience, to do battle for Christ the Lord, the true King.

In the first place, beg of Him by most earnest prayer, that He perfect whatever good thou dost begin, in order that He who hath been pleased to count us in the number of His children, need never be grieved at our evil deeds. For we ought at all times so to serve Him with the good things which He hath given us, that He may not, like an angry father, disinherit his children, nor, like a dread lord, enraged at our evil deeds, hand us over to everlasting punishment as most wicked servants, who would not follow Him to glory.

Let us then rise at length, since the Scripture arouseth us, saying: "It is now the hour for us to rise from sleep" (Rom 13:11); and having opened our eyes to the deifying light, let us hear with awestruck ears what the divine voice, crying out daily, doth admonish us, saying: "Today, if you shall hear his voice, harden not your hearts" (Ps 94[95]:8). And again: "He that hath ears to hear let him hear what the Spirit saith to the churches" (Rev 2:7). And what doth He say?—"Come, children, hearken unto me, I will teach you the fear of the Lord" (Ps 33[34]:12). "Run whilst you have the light of life, that the darkness of death overtake you not" (Jn 12:35).

And the Lord seeking His workman in the multitude of the people, to whom He proclaimeth these words, saith again: "Who is the man that desireth life and loveth to see good days" (Ps 33[34]:13)? If hearing this thou answerest, "I am he," God saith to thee: "If thou wilt have true and everlasting life, keep thy tongue from evil, and thy lips from speaking guile; turn away from evil and do good; seek after peace and pursue it" (Ps 33[34]:14–15). And when you shall have done these things, my eyes shall be upon you, and my ears unto your prayers. And before you shall call upon me I will say: "Behold, I am here" (Is 58:9).

What, dearest brethren, can be sweeter to us than this voice of the Lord inviting us? See, in His loving kindness, the Lord showeth us the way of life. Therefore, having our loins girt with faith and the performance of good works, let us walk His ways under the guidance of the Gospel, that we may be found worthy of seeing Him who hath called us to His kingdom (cf 1 Thes 2:12).

If we desire to dwell in the tabernacle of His kingdom, we

cannot reach it in any way, unless we run thither by good works. But let us ask the Lord with the Prophet, saying to Him: "Lord, who shall dwell in Thy tabernacle, or who shall rest in Thy holy hill" (Ps 14[15]:1)?

After this question, brethren, let us listen to the Lord answering and showing us the way to this tabernacle, saying: "He that walketh without blemish and worketh justice; he that speaketh truth in his heart; who hath not used deceit in his tongue, nor hath done evil to his neighbor, nor hath taken up a reproach against his neighbor" (Ps 14[15]:2–3), who hath brought to naught the foul demon tempting him, casting him out of his heart with his temptation, and hath taken his evil thoughts whilst they were yet weak and hath dashed them against Christ (cf Ps 14[15]:4; Ps 136[137]:9); who fearing the Lord are not puffed up by their goodness of life, but holding that the actual good which is in them cannot be done by themselves, but by the Lord, they praise the Lord working in them (cf Ps 14[15]:4), saying with the Prophet: "Not to us, O Lord, not to us; by to Thy name give glory" (Ps 113[115:1]:9). Thus also the Apostle Paul hath not taken to himself any credit for his preaching, saying: "By the grace of God, I am what I am" (1 Cor 15:10). And again he saith: "He that glorieth, let him glory in the Lord" (2 Cor 10:17).

Hence, the Lord also saith in the Gospel: "He that heareth these my words and doeth them, shall be likened to a wise man who built his house upon a rock; the floods came, the winds blew, and they beat upon that house, and it fell not, for it was founded on a rock" (Mt 7:24–25). The Lord fulfilling these words waiteth for us from day to day, that we respond to His holy admonitions by our works. Therefore, our days are lengthened to a truce for the amendment of the misdeeds of our present life; as the Apostle saith: "Knowest thou not that the patience of God leadeth thee to penance" (Rom 2:4)? For the good Lord saith: "I will not the death of the sinner, but that he be converted and live" (Ezek 33:11).

Now, brethren, that we have asked the Lord who it is that shall dwell in His tabernacle, we have heard the conditions for dwelling there; and if we fulfil the duties of tenants, we shall be heirs of the kingdom of heaven. Our hearts and our bodies must, therefore, be ready to do battle under the biddings of holy obedience; and let us ask the Lord that He supply by the help of His grace what is impossible to us by nature. And if, flying from the pains of hell, we desire to reach life everlasting, then, while there is yet time, and we are still in the flesh, and are able during the present life to fulfil all these things, we must make haste to do now what will profit us forever.

We are, therefore, about to found a school of the Lord's service, in which we hope to introduce nothing harsh or burdensome. But even if, to correct vices or to preserve charity, sound reason dictateth anything that turneth out somewhat stringent, do not at once fly in dismay from the way of salvation, the beginning of which cannot but be narrow. But as we advance in the religious life and faith, we shall run the way of God's commandments with expanded hearts and unspeakable sweetness of love; so that never departing from His guidance and persevering in the monastery in His doctrine till death, we may by patience share in the sufferings of Christ, and be found worthy to be coheirs with Him of His kingdom.

CHAPTER II
What Kind of Man the Abbot Ought to Be

The Abbot who is worthy to be over a monastery, ought always to be mindful of what he is called, and make his works square with his name of Superior. For he is believed to hold the place of Christ in the monastery, when he is called by his name, according to the saying of the Apostle: "You have received the spirit of adoption of sons, whereby we cry *Abba* (Father)" (Rom 8:15). Therefore, the Abbot should never teach, prescribe, or command (which God forbid) anything contrary to the laws of the Lord; but his commands and teaching should be instilled like a leaven of divine justice into the minds of his disciples.

Let the Abbot always bear in mind that he must give an account in the dread judgment of God of both his own teaching and of the obedience of his disciples. And let the Abbot know that whatever lack of profit the master of the house shall find in the sheep, will be laid to the blame of the shepherd. On the other hand he will be blameless, if he gave all a shepherd's care to his restless and unruly flock, and took all pains to correct their corrupt manners; so that their shepherd, acquitted at the Lord's judgment seat, may say to the Lord with the Prophet: "I have not hid Thy justice within my heart. I have declared Thy truth and Thy salvation" (Ps 39[40]:11). "But they contemning have despised me" (Is 1:2; Ezek 20:27). Then at length eternal death will be the crushing doom of the rebellious sheep under his charge.

When, therefore, anyone taketh the name of Abbot he should govern his disciples by a twofold teaching; namely, he should show them all that is good and holy by his deeds more than by his words; explain the commandments of God to intelligent disciples by words, but show the divine precepts to the dull and simple by his works. And let him show by his actions, that whatever he teacheth his disciples as being contrary to the law of God must not be done, "lest perhaps when he hath preached to others, he himself should become a castaway" (1 Cor 9:27), and he himself committing sin, God one day say to him: "Why dost thou declare My justices, and take My covenant in thy mouth? But thou hast hated discipline, and hast cast My words behind thee" (Ps 49[50]:16–17). And: "Thou who sawest the mote in thy brother's eye, hast not seen the beam in thine own" (Mt 7:3).

Let him make no distinction of persons in the monastery. Let him not love one more than another, unless it be one whom he findeth more exemplary in good works and obedience. Let not a free-born be preferred to a freedman, unless there be some other reasonable cause. But if from a just reason the Abbot deemeth it proper to make such a distinction, he may do so in regard to the rank of anyone whomsoever; otherwise let everyone keep his own place; for whether bond or free, we are all one in Christ (cf Gal 3:28; Eph 6:8), and we all bear an equal burden of servitude under one Lord, "for there is no respect of persons with God" (Rom 2:11). We are distinguished with Him in this respect alone, if we are found to excel others in good works and in humility. Therefore, let him have equal charity for all, and impose a uniform discipline for all according to merit.

For in his teaching the Abbot should always observe that principle of the Apostle in which he saith: "Reprove, entreat, rebuke" (2 Tm 4:2), that is, mingling gentleness with severity, as the occasion may call for, let him show the severity of the master and the loving affection of a father. He must sternly rebuke the undisciplined and restless; but he must exhort the obedient, meek, and patient to advance in virtue. But we charge him to rebuke and punish the negligent and haughty. Let him not shut his eyes to the sins of evil-doers; but on their first appearance let him do his utmost to cut them out from the root at once, mindful of the fate of Heli, the priest of Silo (cf 1 Sam 2:11–4:18). The well-disposed and those of good understanding, let him correct at the first and second admonition only with words; but let him chastise the wicked and the hard of heart, and the proud and disobedient at the very first offense with stripes and other bodily punishments, knowing that it is written: "The fool is not corrected with words" (Prov 29:19). And again: "Strike thy son with the rod, and thou shalt deliver his soul from death" (Prov 23:14).

The Abbot ought always to remember what he is and what he is called, and to know that to whom much hath been entrusted, from him much will be required; and let him understand what a difficult and arduous task he assumeth in governing souls and accommodating himself to a variety of characters. Let him so adjust and adapt himself to everyone— to one gentleness of speech, to another by reproofs, and to still another by entreaties, to each one according to his bent and understanding—that he not only suffer no loss in his flock, but may rejoice in the increase of a worthy fold.

Above all things, that the Abbot may not neglect or undervalue the welfare of the souls entrusted to him, let him not have too great a concern about fleeting, earthly, perishable things; but let him always consider that he hath undertaken the government of souls, of which he must give an account. And that he may not perhaps complain of the want of earthly means, let him remember what is written: "Seek ye first the kingdom of God and His justice, and all these things shall be added unto you" (Mt 6:33). And again: "There is no want to them that fear Him" (Ps 33[34]:10). And let him know that he who undertaketh the government of souls must prepare himself to give an account for them; and whatever the number of brethren he hath under his charge, let him be sure that on judgment day he will, without doubt, have to give an account to the Lord for all these souls, in addition to that of his own. And thus, whilst he is in constant fear of the Shepherd's future examination about the sheep entrusted to him, and is watchful of his account for others, he is made solicitous also on his own account; and whilst by his admonitions he had administered correction to others, he is freed from his own failings.

CHAPTER III
Of Calling the Brethren for Counsel

Whenever weighty matters are to be transacted in the monastery, let the Abbot call together the whole community, and make known the matter which is to be considered. Having heard the brethren's views, let him weigh the matter with himself and do what he thinketh best. It is for this reason, however, we said that all should be called for counsel, because the Lord often revealeth to the younger what is best. Let the brethren, however, give their advice with humble submission, and let them not presume stubbornly to defend what seemeth right to them, for it must depend rather on the Abbot's will, so that all obey him in what he considereth best. But as it becometh disciples to obey their master, so also it becometh the master to dispose all things with prudence and justice. Therefore, let all follow the Rule as their guide in everything, and let no one rashly depart from it.

Let no one in the monastery follow the bent of his own heart, and let no one dare to dispute insolently with his Abbot, either inside or outside the monastery. If any one dare to do so, let him be placed under the correction of the Rule. Let the Abbot himself, however, do everything in the fear of the Lord and out of reverence for the Rule, knowing that, beyond a doubt, he will have to give an account to God, the most just Judge, for all his rulings. If, however, matters of less importance, having to do with the welfare of the monastery, are to be treated of, let him use the counsel of the Seniors only, as it is written: "Do all things with counsel, and thou shalt not repent when thou hast done" (Sir 32:24).

CHAPTER IV
The Instruments of Good Works

(1) In the first place to love the Lord God with the whole heart, the whole soul, the whole strength . . .

(2) Then, one's neighbor as one's self (cf Mt 22:37–39; Mk 12:30–31; Lk 10:27).

(3) Then, not to kill . . .

(4) Not to commit adultery . . .

(5) Not to steal . . .

(6) Not to covet (cf Rom 13:9).

(7) Not to bear false witness (cf Mt 19:18; Mk 10:19; Lk 18:20).

(8) To honor all men (cf 1 Pt 2:17).

(9) And what one would not have done to himself, not to do to another (cf Tob 4:16; Mt 7:12; Lk 6:31).

(10) To deny one's self in order to follow Christ (cf Mt 16:24; Lk 9:23).

(11) To chastise the body (cf 1 Cor 9:27).

(12) Not to seek after pleasures.

(13) To love fasting.

(14) To relieve the poor.

(15) To clothe the naked . . .

(16) To visit the sick (cf Mt 25:36).

(17) To bury the dead.

(18) To help in trouble.

(19) To console the sorrowing.

(20) To hold one's self aloof from worldly ways.

(21) To prefer nothing to the love of Christ.

(22) Not to give way to anger.

(23) Not to foster a desire for revenge.

(24) Not to entertain deceit in the heart.

(25) Not to make a false peace.

(26) Not to forsake charity.

(27) Not to swear, lest perchance one swear falsely.

(28) To speak the truth with heart and tongue.

(29) Not to return evil for evil (cf 1 Thes 5:15; 1 Pt 3:9).

(30) To do no injury, yea, even patiently to bear the injury done us.

(31) To love one's enemies (cf Mt 5:44; Lk 6:27).

(32) Not to curse them that curse us, but rather to bless them.

(33) To bear persecution for justice sake (cf Mt 5:10).

(34) Not to be proud . . .

(35) Not to be given to wine (cf Ti 1:7; 1 Tm 3:3).

(36) Not to be a great eater.

(37) Not to be drowsy.

(38) Not to be slothful (cf Rom 12:11).

(39) Not to be a murmurer.

(40) Not to be a detractor.

(41) To put one's trust in God.

(42) To refer what good one sees in himself, not to self, but to God.

(43) But as to any evil in himself, let him be convinced that it is his own and charge it to himself.

(44) To fear the day of judgment.

(45) To be in dread of hell.

(46) To desire eternal life with all spiritual longing.

(47) To keep death before one's eyes daily.

(48) To keep a constant watch over the actions of our life.

(49) To hold as certain that God sees us everywhere.

(50) To dash at once against Christ the evil thoughts which rise in one's heart.

(51) And to disclose them to our spiritual father.

(52) To guard one's tongue against bad and wicked speech.

(53) Not to love much speaking.

(54) Not to speak useless words and such as provoke laughter.

(55) Not to love much or boisterous laughter.

(56) To listen willingly to holy reading.

(57) To apply one's self often to prayer.

(58) To confess one's past sins to God daily in prayer with sighs and tears, and to amend them for the future.

(59) Not to fulfil the desires of the flesh (cf Gal 5:16).

(60) To hate one's own will.

(61) To obey the commands of the Abbot in all things, even though he himself (which Heaven forbid) act otherwise, mindful of that precept of the Lord: "What they say, do ye; what they do, do ye not" (Mt 23:3).

(62) Not to desire to be called holy before one is; but to be holy first, that one may be truly so called.

(63) To fulfil daily the commandments of God by works.

(64) To love chastity.

(65) To hate no one.

(66) Not to be jealous; not to entertain envy.

(67) Not to love strife.

(68) Not to love pride.

(69) To honor the aged.

(70) To love the younger.

(71) To pray for one's enemies in the love of Christ.

(72) To make peace with an adversary before the setting of the sun.

(73) And never to despair of God's mercy.

Behold, these are the instruments of the spiritual art, which, if they have been applied without ceasing day and night and approved on judgment day, will merit for us from the Lord that reward which He hath promised: "The eye hath not seen, nor the ear heard, neither hath it entered into the heart of man, what things God hath prepared for them that love Him" (1 Cor 2:9). But the workshop in which we perform all these works with diligence is the enclosure of the monastery, and stability in the community.

CHAPTER V
Of Obedience

The first degree of humility is obedience without delay. This becometh those who, on account of the holy subjection which they have promised, or of the fear of hell, or the glory of life everlasting, hold nothing dearer than Christ. As soon as anything hath been commanded by the Superior they permit no delay in the execution, as if the matter had been commanded by God Himself. Of these the Lord saith: "At the hearing of the ear he hath obeyed Me" (Ps 17[18]:45). And again He saith to the teachers: "He that heareth you heareth Me" (Lk 10:16).

Such as these, therefore, instantly quitting their own work and giving up their own will, with hands disengaged, and leaving unfinished what they were doing, follow up, with the ready step of obedience, the work of command with deeds; and thus, as if in the same moment, both matters—the master's command and the disciple's finished work—are, in the swiftness of the fear of God, speedily finished together, whereunto the desire of advancing to eternal life urgeth them. They, therefore, seize upon the narrow way whereof the Lord saith: "Narrow is the way which leadeth to life" (Mt 7:14), so that, not living according to their own desires and pleasures but walking according to the judgment and will of another, they live in monasteries, and desire an Abbot to be over them. Such as these truly live up to the maxim of the Lord in which He saith: "I came not to do My own will, but the will of Him that sent Me" (Jn 6:38).

This obedience, however, will be acceptable to God and agreeable to men then only, if what is commanded is done without hesitation, delay, lukewarmness, grumbling, or complaint, because the obedience which is rendered to Superiors is rendered to God. For He Himself hath said: "He that heareth you heareth Me" (Lk 10:16). And it must be rendered by the disciples with a good will, "for the Lord loveth a cheerful giver" (2 Cor 9:7). For if the disciple obeyeth with an ill will, and murmureth, not only with lips but also in his heart, even though he fulfil the command, yet it will not be acceptable to God, who regardeth the heart of the murmurer. And for such an action he acquireth no reward; rather he incurreth the penalty of murmurers, unless he maketh satisfactory amendment.

CHAPTER XXI
Of the Deans of the Monastery

If the brotherhood is large, let brethren of good repute and holy life be chosen from among them and be appointed Deans; and let them take care of their deaneries in everything according to the commandments of God and the directions of their Abbot. Let such be chosen Deans as the Abbot may safely trust to share his burden. Let them not be chosen for their rank, but for the merit of their life and their wisdom and knowledge; and if any of them, puffed up with pride, should be found blameworthy and, after having been corrected once and again and even a third time, refuseth to amend, let him be deposed, and one who is worthy be placed in his stead. We make the same regulation with reference to the Prior.

CHAPTER XXIII
Of Excommunication for Faults

If a brother is found stubborn or disobedient or proud or murmuring, or opposed to anything in the Holy Rule and a contemner of the commandments of his Superiors, let him be admonished by his Superiors once and again in secret, according to the command of our Lord (cf Mt 18:15–16). If he doth not amend let him be taken to task publicly before all. But if he doth not reform even then, and he understandeth what a penalty it is, let him be placed under excommunication; but if even then he remaineth obstinate let him undergo corporal punishment.

CHAPTER XXIV
What the Manner of Excommunication Should Be

The degree of excommunication or punishment ought to be meted out according to the gravity of the offense, and to determine that is left to the judgment of the Abbot. If, however, anyone of the brethren is detected in smaller faults, let him be debarred from eating at the common table.

The following shall be the practice respecting one who is excluded from the common table: that he does not intone a psalm or an antiphon nor read a lesson in the oratory until he hath made satisfaction; let him take his meal alone, after the refection of the brethren; thus: if, for instance, the brethren take their meal at the sixth hour that brother will take his at the ninth, and if the brethren take theirs at the ninth, he will take his in the evening, until by due satisfaction he obtaineth pardon.

CHAPTER XXV
Of Graver Faults

But let the brother who is found guilty of a graver fault be excluded from both the table and the oratory. Let none of the brethren join his company or speak with him. Let him be alone at the work enjoined on him, persevering in penitential sorrow, mindful of the terrible sentence of the Apostle who saith, that "such a man is delivered over for the destruction of the flesh, that the spirit may be saved in the day of the Lord" (1 Cor 5:5). Let him get his food alone in such quantity and at such a time as the Abbot shall deem fit; and let him not be blessed by anyone passing by, nor the food that is given him.

CHAPTER XXVII
How Concerned the Abbot Should Be about the Excommunicated

Let the Abbot show all care and concern towards offending brethren because "they that are in health need not a physician, but they that are sick" (Mt 9:12). Therefore, like a prudent physician he ought to use every opportunity to send consolers, namely, discreet elderly brethren, to console the wavering brother, as it were, in secret, and induce him to make humble satisfaction; and let them cheer him up "lest he be swallowed up with overmuch sorrow" (2 Cor 2:7); but, as the same Apostle saith, "confirm your charity towards him" (2 Cor 2:8); and let prayer be said for him by all.

The Abbot must take the utmost pains, and strive with all prudence and zeal, that none of the flock entrusted to him perish. For the Abbot must know that he has taken upon himself the care of infirm souls, not a despotism over the strong; and let him fear the threat of the Prophet wherein the Lord saith: "What ye saw to be fat, that ye took to yourselves, and what was diseased you threw away" (Ezek 34:3–4). And let him follow the loving example of the Good Shepherd, who, leaving the ninety-nine sheep on the mountains, went to seek the one that had gone astray, on whose weakness He had such pity, that He was pleased to lay it on His sacred shoulders and thus carry it back to the fold (cf Lk 15:5).

CHAPTER XXXI
The Kind of Man the Cellarer of the Monastery Ought to Be

Let there be chosen from the brotherhood as Cellarer of the monastery a wise man, of settled habits, temperate and frugal, not conceited, irritable, resentful, sluggish, or wasteful, but fearing God, who may be as a father to the whole brotherhood.

Let him have the charge of everything, let him do nothing without the command of the Abbot, let him do what hath been ordered him and not grieve the brethren. If a brother should perchance request anything of him unreasonably let him not sadden the brother with a cold refusal, but politely and with humility refuse him who asketh amiss. Let him be watchful of his own soul, always mindful of the saying of the Apostle: "For they that have ministered well, shall purchase to themselves a good degree" (1 Tm 3:13). Let him provide for the sick, the children, the guests, and the poor, with all care, knowing that, without doubt, he will have to give an account of all these things on judgment day. Let him regard all the vessels of the monastery and all its substance, as if they were sacred vessels of the altar. Let him neglect nothing and let him not give way to avarice, nor let him be wasteful and a squanderer of the goods of the monastery; but let him do all things in due measure and according to the bidding of his Abbot.

Above all things, let him be humble; and if he hath not the things to give, let him answer with a kind word, because it is written: "A good word is above the best gift" (Sir 18:17). Let him have under his charge everything that the Abbot hath entrusted to him, and not presume to meddle with matters forbidden him. Let him give the brethren their apportioned allowance without a ruffle or delay, that they may not be scandalized, mindful of what the Divine Word declareth that he deserveth who shall scandalize one of these little ones: "It were better for him that a millstone were hanged about his neck and that he were drowned in the depth of the sea" (Mt 18:6).

If the community is large, let assistants be given him, that, with their help, he too may fulfil the office entrusted to him with an even temper. Let the things that are to be given be distributed, and the things that are to be gotten asked for at the proper times, so that nobody may be disturbed or grieved in the house of God.

CHAPTER XLVIII
Of the Daily Work

Idleness is the enemy of the soul; and therefore the brethren ought to be employed in manual labor at certain times, at others, in devout reading. Hence, we believe that the time for each will be properly ordered by the following arrangement; namely, that from Easter till the calends of October, they go out in the morning from the first till about the fourth hour, to do the necessary work, but that from the fourth till about the sixth hour they devote to reading. After the sixth hour, however, when they have risen from table, let them rest in their beds in complete silence; or if, perhaps, anyone desireth to read for himself, let him so read that he doth not disturb others. Let None be said somewhat earlier, about the middle of the eighth hour; and then let them work again at what is necessary until Vespers.

If, however, the needs of the place, or poverty should require that they do the work of gathering the harvest themselves, let them not be downcast, for then are they monks in truth, if they live by the work of their hands, as did also our forefathers and the Apostles. However, on account of the faint-hearted let all things be done with moderation.

From the calends of October till the beginning of Lent, let them apply themselves to reading until the second hour complete. At the second hour let Tierce be said, and then let all be employed in the work which hath been assigned to them till the ninth hour. When, however, the first signal for the hour of None hath been given, let each one leave off from work and be ready when the second signal shall strike. But after their repast let them devote themselves to reading or the psalms.

During the Lenten season let them be employed in reading

from morning until the third hour, and till the tenth hour let them do the work which is imposed on them. During these days of Lent let all receive books from the library, and let them read them through in order. These books are to be given out at the beginning of the Lenten season.

Above all, let one or two of the seniors be appointed to go about the monastery during the time that the brethren devote to reading and take notice, lest perhaps a slothful brother be found who giveth himself up to idleness or vain talk, and doth not attend to his reading, and is unprofitable, not only to himself, but disturbeth also others. If such a one be found (which God forbid), let him be punished once and again. If he doth not amend, let him come under the correction of the Rule in such a way that others may fear. And let not brother join brother at undue times.

On Sunday also let all devote themselves to reading, except those who are appointed to the various functions. But if anyone should be so careless and slothful that he will not or cannot meditate or read, let some work be given him to do, that he may not be idle.

Let such work or charge be given to the weak and the sickly brethren, that they are neither idle, nor so wearied with the strain of work that they are driven away. Their weakness must be taken into account by the Abbot.

CHAPTER LIII
Of the Reception of Guests

Let all guests who arrive be received as Christ, because He will say: "I was a stranger and you took Me in" (Mt 25:35). And let due honor be shown to all, especially to those "of the household of the faith" (Gal 6:10) and to wayfarers.

When, therefore, a guest is announced, let him be met by the Superior and the brethren with every mark of charity. And let them first pray together, and then let them associate with one another in peace. This kiss of peace should not be given before a prayer hath first been said, on account of satanic deception. In the greeting let all humility be shown to the guests, whether coming or going; with the head bowed down or the whole body prostrate on the ground, let Christ be adored in them as He is also received.

When the guests have been received, let them be accompanied to prayer, and after that let the Superior, or whom he shall bid, sit down with them. Let the divine law be read to the guest that he may be edified, after which let every kindness be shown him. Let the fast be broken by the Superior in deference to the guest, unless, perchance, it be a day of solemn fast, which cannot be broken. Let the brethren, however, keep the customary fast. Let the Abbot pour the water on the guest's hands, and let both the Abbot and the whole brotherhood wash the feet of all the guests. When they have been washed, let them say this verse: "We have received Thy mercy, O God, in the midst of Thy temple" (Ps 47[48]:10). Let the greatest care be taken, especially in the reception of the poor and travelers, because Christ is received more specially in them; whereas regard for the wealthy itself procureth them respect.

Let the kitchen of the Abbot and the guests be apart, that the brethren may not be disturbed by the guests who arrive at uncertain times and who are never wanting in the monastery. Let two brothers who are able to fulfil this office well go into the kitchen for a year. Let help be given them as they need it, that they may serve without murmuring; and when they have not enough to do, let them go out again for work where it is commanded them. Let this course be followed, not only in this office, but in all the offices of the monastery—that whenever the brethren need help, it be given them, and that when they have nothing to do, they again obey orders. Moreover, let also a God-fearing brother have assigned to him the apartment of the guests, where there should be sufficient number of beds made up; and let the house of God be wisely managed by the wise.

On no account let anyone who is not ordered to do so, associate or speak with guests; but if he meet or see them, having saluted them humbly, as we have said, and asked a blessing, let him pass on saying that he is not allowed to speak with a guest.

CHAPTER LVIII
Of the Manner of Admitting Brethren

Let easy admission not be given to one who newly cometh to change his life; but, as the Apostle saith, "Try the spirits, whether they be of God" (1 Jn 4:1). If, therefore, the newcomer keepeth on knocking, and after four or five days it is seen that he patiently beareth the harsh treatment offered him and the difficulty of admission, and that he persevereth in his request, let admission be granted him, and let him live for a few days in the apartment of the guests.

But afterward let him live in the apartment of novices, and there let him meditate, eat, and sleep. Let a senior also be appointed for him, who is qualified to win souls, who will observe him with great care and see whether he really seeketh God, whether he is eager for the Work of God, obedience and humiliations. Let him be shown all the hard and rugged things through which we pass on to God.

If he promiseth to remain steadfast, let this Rule be read to him in order after the lapse of two months, and let it be said to him: Behold the law under which thou desirest to combat. If thou canst keep it, enter; if, however, thou canst not, depart freely. If he still persevereth, then let him be taken back to the aforesaid apartment of the novices, and let him be tried again in all patience. And after the lapse of six months let the Rule be read over to him, that he may know for what purpose he entereth. And if he still remaineth firm, let the same Rule be read to him again after four months. And if, after having weighed the matter with himself he promiseth to keep everything, and to do everything that is commanded him, then let him be received into the community, knowing that he is now placed under the law of the Rule, and that from that day forward it is no longer permitted to him to wrest his neck from under the yoke of the Rule, which after so long a deliberation he was at liberty either to refuse or to accept.

Let him who is received promise in the oratory, in the presence of all, before God and His saints, stability, the conversion of morals, and obedience, in order that, if he should ever do otherwise, he may know that he will be condemned by God "Whom he mocketh." Let him make a written statement of his promise in the name of the saints whose relics are there, and of the Abbot there present. Let him write this document with his own hand; or at least, if he doth not know how to write, let another write it at his request, and let the novice make his mark, and with his own hand place it on the altar. When he hath placed it there, let the novice next begin the verse: "Uphold me, O Lord, according to Thy word and I shall live; and let me not be confounded in my expectations" (Ps 118[119]:116). Then let all the brotherhood repeat this verse three times, adding the *Gloria Patri*.

Then let that novice brother cast himself down at the feet of all, that they may pray for him; and from that day let him be counted in the brotherhood. If he hath any property, let him first either dispose of it to the poor or bestow it on the monastery by a formal donation, reserving nothing for himself as indeed he should know that from that day onward he will no longer have power even over his own body.

Let him, therefore, be divested at once in the oratory of the garments with which he is clothed, and be vested in the garb of the monastery. But let the clothes of which he was divested be laid by in the wardrobe to be preserved, that, if on the devil's suasion he should ever consent to leave the monastery (which God forbid) he be then stripped of his monastic habit and cast out. But let him not receive the document of his profession which the Abbot took from the altar, but let it be preserved in the monastery.

CHAPTER LXIII
Of the Order in the Monastery

Let all keep their order in the monastery in such wise, that the time of their conversion and the merit of their life distinguish it, or as the Abbot hath directed. Let the Abbot not disorder the flock committed to him, nor by an arbitrary use of his power dispose of anything unjustly; but let him always bear in mind that he will have to give an account to God of all his judgments and works. Hence in the order that he hath established, or that the brethren had, let them approach for the kiss of peace, for Communion, intone the psalms, and stand in choir.

And in no place whatever let age determine the order or be a disadvantage; because Samuel and Daniel when mere boys judged the priests (cf 1 Sam 3; Dan 13:44–62). Excepting those, therefore, whom, as we have said, the Abbot from higher motives hath advanced, or, for certain reasons, hath lowered, let all the rest take their place as they are converted: thus, for instance, let him who came into the monastery at the second hour of the day, know that he is younger than he who came at the first hour, whatever his age or dignity may be.

Children are to be kept under discipline at all times and by everyone. Therefore, let the younger honor their elders, and the older love the younger.

In naming each other let no one be allowed to address another by his simple name; but let the older style the younger brethren, brothers; let the younger, however, call their elders, fathers, by which is implied the reverence due to a father. But because the Abbot is believed to hold the place of Christ, let him be styled Lord and Abbot, not only by assumption on his part, but out of love and reverence for Christ. Let him think of this and so show himself, that he be worthy of such an honor. Wherever, then, the brethren meet each other, let the younger ask the blessing from the older; and when the older passeth by, let the younger rise and give him place to sit; and let the younger not presume to sit down with him unless his elder biddeth him to do so, that it may be done as it is written: "In honor preventing one another" (Rom 12:10).

Let children and boys take their places in the oratory and at table with all due discipline; outdoors, however, or wherever they may be, let them be under custody and discipline until they reach the age of understanding.

CHAPTER LXIV
Of the Election of the Abbot

In the election of an Abbot let this always be observed as a rule, that he be placed in the position whom the whole community with one consent, in the fear of God, or even a small part, with sounder judgment, shall elect. But let him who is to be elected be chosen for the merit of his life and the wisdom of his doctrine, though he be the last in the community.

But even if the whole community should by mutual consent elect a man who agreeth to connive at their evil ways (which God forbid) and these irregularities in some come to the knowledge of the Bishop to whose diocese the place belongeth, or to neighboring Abbots, or Christian people, let them not permit the intrigue of the wicked to succeed, but let them appoint a worthy steward over the house of God, knowing that they shall receive a bountiful reward for this action, if they do it with a pure intention and godly zeal; whereas, on the other hand, they commit a sin if they neglect it.

But when the Abbot hath been elected let him bear in mind how great a burden he hath taken upon himself, and to whom he must give an account of his stewardship (cf Lk 16:2); and let him be convinced that it becometh him better to serve than to rule. He must, therefore, be versed in the divine law, that he may know whence "to bring forth new things and old" (Mt 13:52). Let him be chaste, sober, and merciful, and let him always exalt "mercy above judgment" (Jas 2:13), that he also may obtain mercy.

Let him hate vice, but love the brethren. And even in his corrections, let him act with prudence and not go to extremes, lest, while he aimeth to remove the rust too thoroughly, the vessel be broken. Let him always keep his own frailty in mind, and remember that "the bruised reed must not be broken" (Is 42:3). In this we are not saying that he should allow evils to take root, but that he cut them off with prudence and charity, as he shall see it is best for each one, as we have already said; and let him aim to be loved rather than feared.

Let him not be fussy or over-anxious, exacting, or head-strong; let him not be jealous or suspicious, because he will never have rest. In all his commands, whether they refer to things spiritual or temporal, let him be cautious and consid-erate. Let him be discerning and temperate in the tasks which he enjoineth, recalling the discretion of holy Jacob who saith: "If I should cause my flocks to be overdriven, they would all die in one day" (Gen 33:13). Keeping in view these and other dic-tates of discretion, the mother of virtues, let him so temper everything that the strong may still have something to desire and the weak may not draw back. Above all, let him take heed that he keep this Rule in all its detail; that when he hath served well he may hear from the Lord what the good servant heard who gave his fellow-servants bread in season: "Amen, I say to you," He saith, "he shall set him over all his goods" (Mt 24:47).

CHAPTER LXXII
Of the Virtuous Zeal Which the Monks Ought to Have

As there is a harsh and evil zeal which separateth from God and leadeth to hell, so there is a virtuous zeal which separateth from vice and leadeth to God and life everlasting.

Let the monks, therefore, practice this zeal with most ardent love; namely, that in honor they forerun one another (cf Rom 12:10). Let them bear their infirmities, whether of body or mind, with the utmost patience; let them vie with one another in obedience. Let no one follow what he thinketh useful to himself, but rather to another. Let them practice fraternal charity with a chaste love.

Let them fear God and love their Abbot with sincere and humble affection; let them prefer nothing whatever to Christ, and may He lead us all together to life everlasting.

Endnotes

Preface

1. Information about the life of St. Benedict was obtained from several sources including, *The Rule of St. Benedict,* translated by Anthony C. Meisel and M. L. del Mastro (New York: Image Books, 1975); *New Advent Catholic Encyclopedia,* 2nd ed., H. Bettenson, ed, "Documents of the Christian Church" (London: Oxford University Press, 1971); and *The Mystical Theology of the Eastern Church,* by Vladimir Lossky (Cambridge: James Clarke & Co, 1957).

Chapter 4: The Rule of Focused and Independent Ventures

1. Benedict borrowed and modified several passages from Pachomius in developing his own Rule.

Chapter 11: The Rule of Counsel

1. See I. McLean and H. Lorrey, "Voting in Medieval Universities and Religious Orders." Paper presented at the conference on Rules of the Game of Politics in the Middle Ages and the Renaissance, at UCLA, March, 2001.

2. The Dominican monks of the thirteenth century fine-tuned the process of impeachment in their order's constitution. There were four acceptable reasons for impeachment:

 177

crime, causing disunity to the order, inept administration, and inability to perform his services through illness, etc. Generally a request for resignation would be tendered prior to the actual impeachment (see note 1 above). Other interesting sources consulted for this chapter include "Electing Popes: Approval Balloting and Qualified-Majority Rule Colomer" by J. and I. McLean, *Journal of Interdisciplinary History* 29(1): 1–12; and *Theory of Voting* by Robin Farquharson (Oxford: Backwell, 1969).

Chapter 13: The Rule of Leader Example

1. See L. Frank Baum, *Ozma of Oz* (Chicago: The Reilly & Lee Co., 1907), pp. 232–33.

Appendix I

1. See Panayiotis Christou, "The Monastic Life in the Eastern Orthodox Church," in *The Orthodox Ethos: Studies in Orthodoxy*, Vol. 1, ed. A. J. Philippou (Oxford: Holywell Press, 1964).

Appendix II

1. See François Pierre Guillaume Guizot, *General History of Civilization in Modern Europe*, Vol. 2, translated by William Hazlitt (New York, Boston: H. M. Caldwell Co., 1846) p. 75.
2. See E. J. Mayeaux Jr., History of Western Medicine and Surgery, 1989, *http://lib-sh.lsumc.edu/fammed/grounds/history.html*, p. 3.

About the Authors

Craig Galbraith is currently a professor of entrepreneurship and technology at the Cameron School of Business, University of North Carolina, Wilmington. He is also a managing partner of Galbraith, Galbraith & Merrill, a firm that specializes in business valuation and business plan development with offices in La Jolla, California, and in North Carolina. Dr. Galbraith has been a consultant to a variety of firms, from small high-technology start-ups to *Fortune* 500 companies.

He received his Ph.D. from Purdue University. Prior to his present university position, at different times he has been a founder and CFO of a start-up biotech firm, a gold miner, and a librarian. During his life he has lived and studied at several Benedictine monasteries. Dr. Galbraith has published a variety of books, ranging in topics from artificial intelligence to entrepreneurship. Dr. Galbraith maintains residences in Pacific Beach, California, and Kure Beach, North Carolina.

Oliver Galbraith III was an award-winning professor emeritus of Decision Sciences and Information Systems at San Diego State University. His interests were in the areas of small business and engineering management, and church leadership. Prior to joining the academic world, he was employed as an industrial engineer by Abbot Laboratories. He received his MBA from Northwestern University, and his Ph.D. from UCLA. Dr. Galbraith had been a consultant to small and large firms, and wrote extensively in the small business management area. He was a combat Army veteran of the European battlefields in World War II and lived in San Diego, California.

While working on the manuscript of this book, Oliver Galbraith III passed away on April 14, 2002. He was seventy-six. All who knew and worked with him will sorely miss Dr. Galbraith's clever wit, scholarly inspiration, and remarkable knowledge of history.